Quilt Notes

Whether or not you have a green thumb when it comes to gardening, you can create beautiful flowers from this collection of scrappy garden quilts. The use of scraps is very appropriate for a garden quilt, since the most beautiful gardens are often a rainbow of color. Sort through your scraps or take a trip to your local fabric store to find your favorite colors to make blooming flowers and fluttering butterflies.

Using the dozen patterns in this book, you can fill your home with garden quilts in various sizes and a variety of colors. This is a garden every quilter will want to watch grow stitch by stitch.

E-mail: Customer_Service@whitebirches.com

SCRAPPY GARDEN QUILTS is published by House of White Birches, 306 East Parr Road, Berne, IN 46711, telephone (260) 589-4000. Printed in USA. Copyright © 2004 House of White Birches.

RETAILERS: If you would like to carry this pattern book or any other House of White Birches publications, call the Wholesale Department at Annie's Attic to set up a direct account: (903) 636-4303. Also, request a complete listing of publications available from House of White Birches.

Every effort has been made to ensure that the instructions in this pattern book are complete and accurate. We cannot, however, take responsibility for human error, typographical mistakes or variations in individual work.

ISBN: 1-59217-042-0

1 2 3 4 5 6 7 8 9

STAFF

Editor: Jeanne Stauffer
Associate Editor: Dianne Schmidt
Technical Editor: Sandra L. Hatch
Technical Artist: Connie Rand
Copy Editors: Michelle Beck, Nicki Lehman, Conor Allen
Art Director: Brad Snow
Assistant Art Director: Karen Allen
Graphic Arts Supervisor: Ronda Bechinski
Graphic Artist: Vicki Staggs, Jessi Butler
Photography: Tammy Christian, Kelly Heydinger, Christena Green
Photo Stylist: Tammy Nussbaum

HOUSE OF WHITE BIRCHES, BERNE, INDIANA 46711   WWW.WHITEBIRCHES.COM   Scrappy Garden Quilts   1

Rose of My Heart

BY RUTH SWASEY

Bali prints have such wonderful shading and surprise highlights. They combine in this pretty heart-shape flower pattern to make a beautiful bed-size quilt.

Project Specifications
Quilt Size: 82" x 96"
Block Size: 14" x 14"
Number of Blocks: 30

Fabric & Batting
- ⅛ yard yellow mottled for flower centers
- ⅔ yard pink Bali print for binding
- 1 yard green Bali print for leaves
- 1 yard dark green Bali print for stems and border
- 2½ yards total 4 different pink Bali prints for flowers
- 6¼ yards white/blue mottled for background
- Batting 88" x 102"
- Backing 88" x 102"

Tools & Supplies
- All-purpose thread to match fabrics
- Quilting thread
- 11 yards fusible web
- 11¾ yards fabric stabilizer
- Basic sewing tools and supplies

Making Appliqué Blocks

1. Cut 30 A squares white/blue mottled 14½" x 14½"; set aside remaining width for borders. Fold each square on both diagonals and crease to mark centers.

Rose of My Heart
14" x 14" Block

2. Prepare templates using patterns given.

3. Bond fusible web to the wrong side of the yellow mottled and pink and green Bali prints and to a ⅓ yard section of dark green Bali print for stems. Trace shapes onto the paper side of the fused fabric referring to patterns for number to cut. Cut out shapes on traced lines; remove paper backing.

4. For each block, begin by placing two leaf shapes (one reversed) on two opposite corners of an A square, 1¼" from corners close to the crease lines as shown in Figure 1; fuse in place.

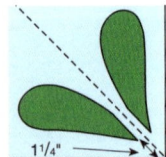

Figure 1
Place 2 leaf shapes
(1 reversed) on 2 opposite
corners of an A square, 1¼"
from corners on the crease line.

5. Center a stem piece on the creased line on top of the fused leaves referring to Figure 2; fuse in place.

Figure 2
Center a stem piece on the creased line on top of the fused leaves.

6. Arrange four heart petals in the center, overlapping in any direction referring to the block drawing and the Placement Diagram; fuse in place. **Note:** *Overlap pieces in different configurations and combine various fabric shades to add variety.* Fuse flower centers over center.

7. Center and fuse a corner heart to the remaining corners of the square to complete fusing; repeat for 30 blocks.

8. Cut 30 squares fabric stabilizer 14" x 14"; pin a square to the wrong side of each fused block.

9. Using all-purpose thread to match fabrics and a machine buttonhole stitch, stitch around each fused shape. When stitching is complete, remove fabric stabilizer.

Completing the Top

1. Arrange the blocks on a flat surface. When satisfied with the layout, join five blocks to make a row; press seams in one direction. Repeat for six rows.

2. Join the rows as planned; press seams in one direction.

3. Cut and piece two 2½" x 74½" M strips and two 2½" x 84½" N strips dark green Bali print. Sew N to opposite sides and M to the top and bottom of the pieced center; press seams toward strips.

4. Cut two 4½" x 88½" O strips and two 4½" x 82½" P strips along length of remaining width of white/blue mottled. Sew O to opposite sides and P to the top and bottom of the pieced center; press seams toward strips.

Finishing the Quilt

1. Sandwich batting between the completed top and prepared backing piece; pin or baste layers together to hold flat for quilting.

2. Quilt as desired by hand or machine. **Note:** *The quilt shown was professionally machine-quilted in an allover design using white quilting thread.*

3. When quilting is complete, trim batting and backing even with quilted top; remove pins or basting.

4. Cut nine 2¼" by fabric width strips pink Bali print; join strips on short ends to make one long strip for binding.

5. Fold the binding strip in half along length with wrong sides together; press.

6. Sew binding strip to quilt edge with raw edges matching, mitering corners and overlapping beginning and end; turn to the backside. Hand- or machine-stitch in place. ■

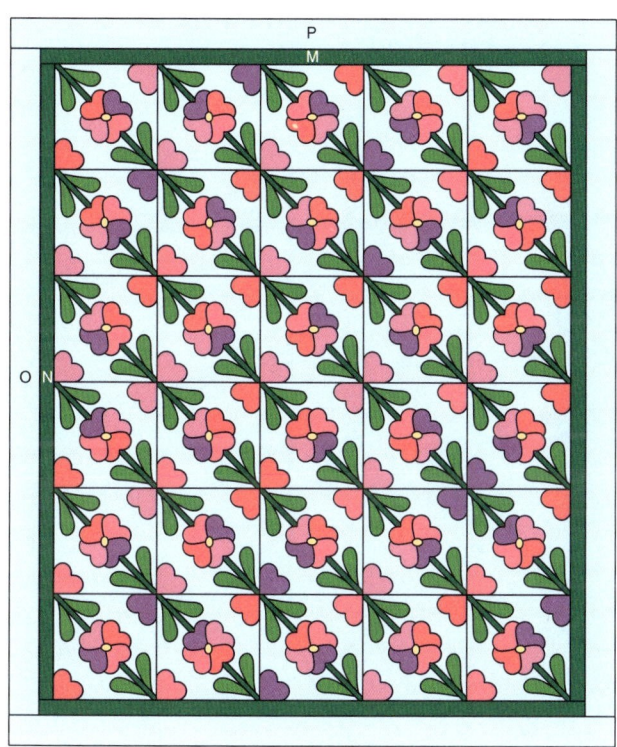

Rose of My Heart
Placement Diagram
82" x 96"

Flower Center
Cut 30 yellow mottled

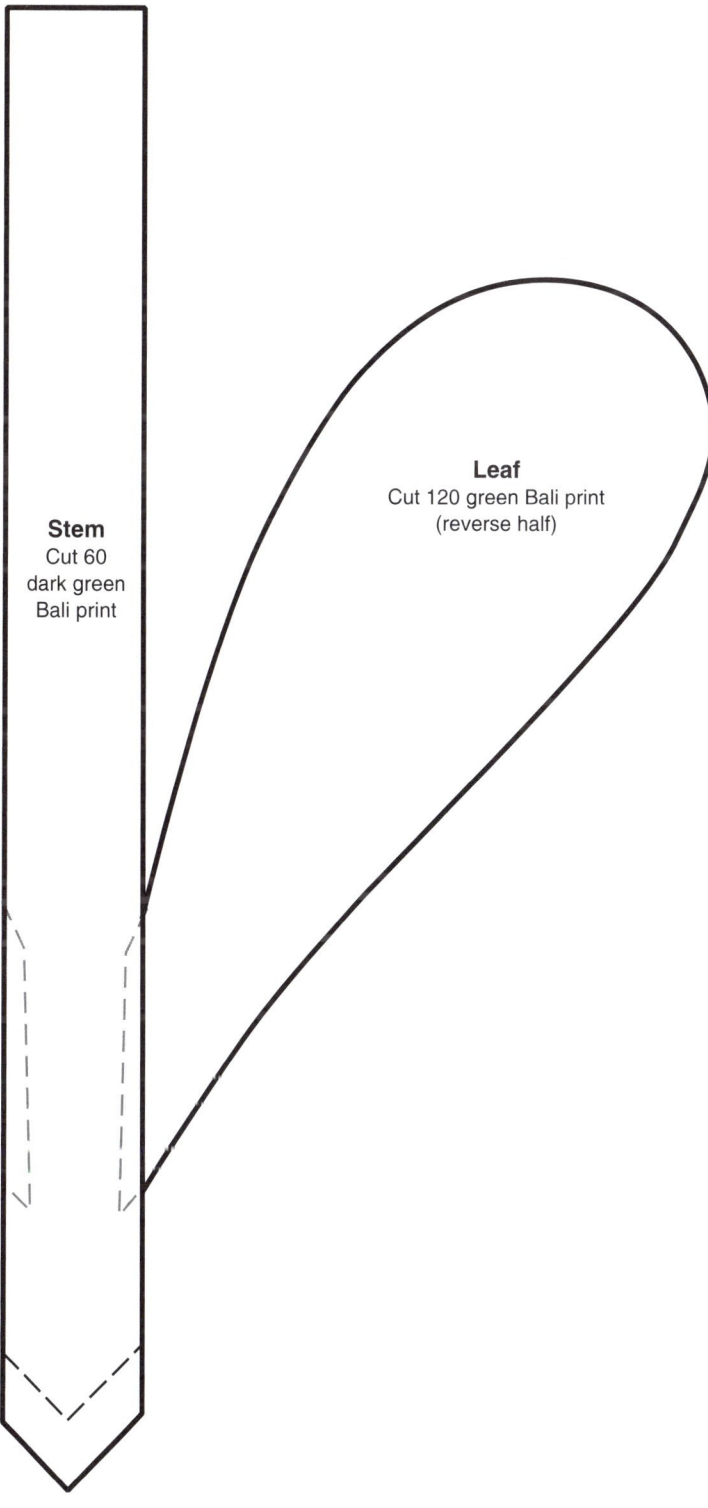

Stem
Cut 60 dark green Bali print

Leaf
Cut 120 green Bali print
(reverse half)

ROSE OF MY HEART

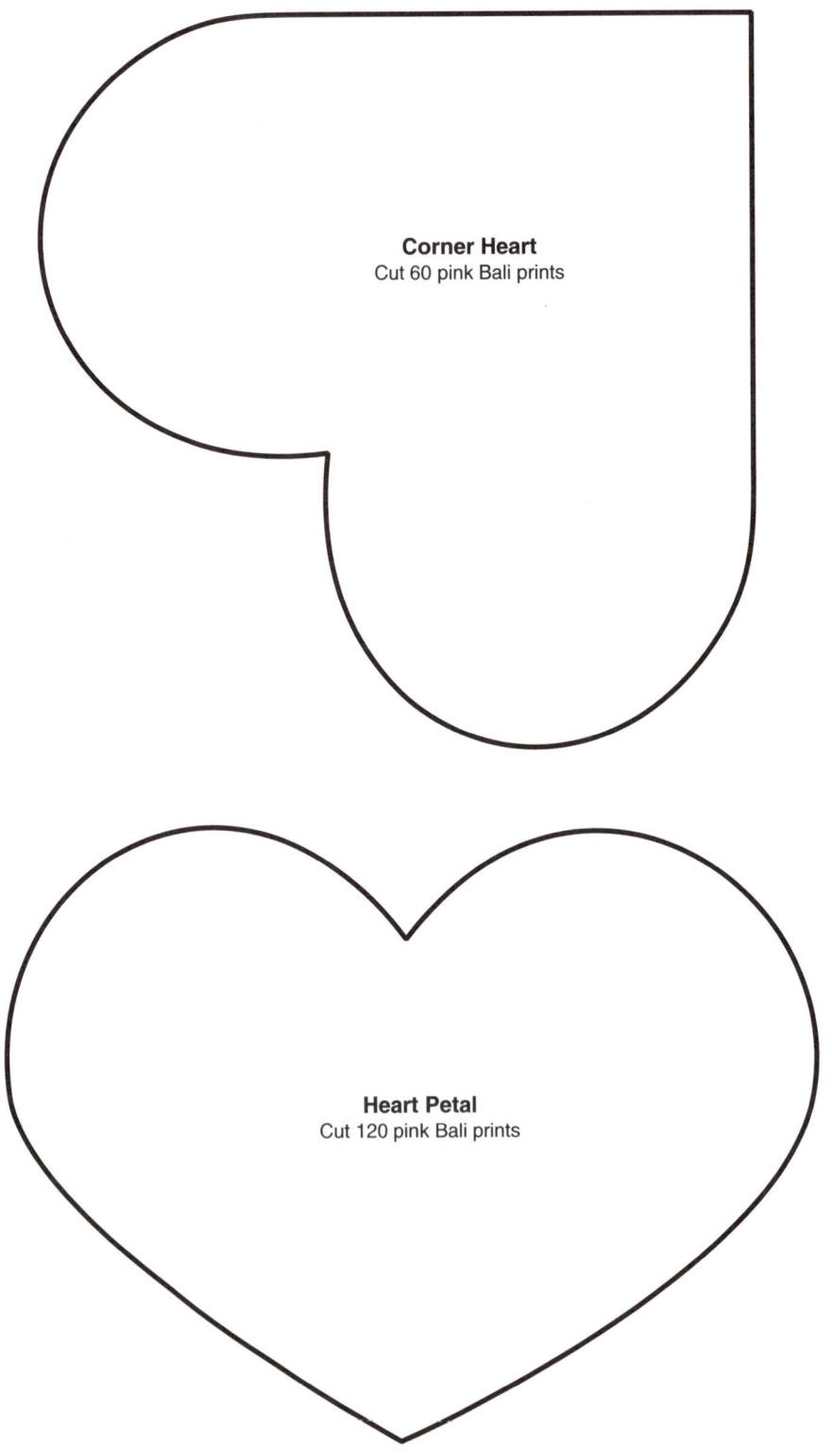

Ramblin' Rose

BY SUE HARVEY

The design of this garden quilt is formed not by the blocks themselves but by the placement of fabrics in the corners of the blocks.

Project Specifications
Quilt Size: 57" x 81"
Block Size: 6" x 6"
Number of Blocks: 96

Fabric & Batting
- ½ yard green plaid
- ½ yard green print
- ½ yard rose print (or enough to cut 156 B triangles)
- ½ yard vine print (or enough to cut 156 B triangles)
- 1 yard burgundy plaid
- 1¼ yards gold plaid
- 4 yards off-white print
- Backing 63" x 87"
- Batting 63" x 87"
- 8 yards self-made or purchased binding

Tools & Supplies
- Coordinating all-purpose thread
- Basic sewing supplies and tools and template plastic

Project Note
It is important to carefully choose the fabric for the rose square inside the green square and the vine square inside the burgundy star. The fabrics must have a design that will form a rose and a vine from the corner triangles when four blocks are combined.

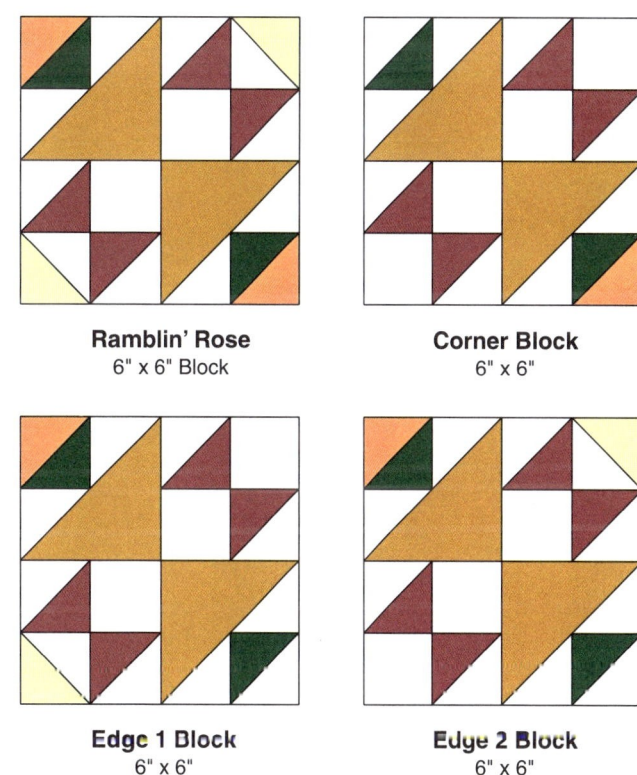

Ramblin' Rose
6" x 6" Block

Corner Block
6" x 6"

Edge 1 Block
6" x 6"

Edge 2 Block
6" x 6"

Instructions
1. Cut two 3½" x 72½" and two 3½" x 48½" border strips along the length of the off-white print; set aside.

2. Prepare templates using pattern pieces given. Cut as directed on each piece, carefully placing B triangles on rose and vine fabrics as shown in Figure 1.

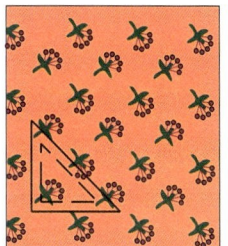

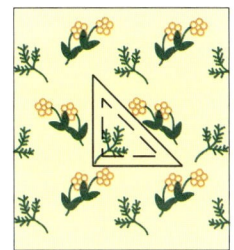

Figure 1
Carefully place B triangle pattern on rose and vine fabrics as shown.

3. Sew pieces together to make units referring to Figure 2 and the Color Key. Press all units.

Block Unit 1
Make 156
Block Unit 2
Make 36
Block Unit 3
Make 152
Block Unit 4
Make 40
B
A
B
A
B
C
B
C

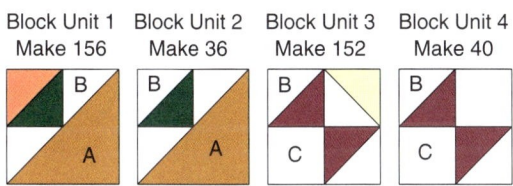

Figure 2
Join pieces to make block units as shown.

4. Join pieced units to make Ramblin' Rose, Corner, Edge 1 and Edge 2 blocks referring to Figure 3 for positioning of units and number of each block to make. Press all blocks.

5. Arrange blocks in 12 rows of eight blocks each referring to Figure 4 and the Placement Diagram for positioning of blocks. Join blocks in rows; join rows to complete pieced center. Press all seams.

6. Referring to Figure 5 and Color Key, make four corner units and 180 B-B units; press.

7. Sew the 3½" x 72½" strips cut in step 1 to opposite long sides of the pieced center; press seams toward strips.

Ramblin' Rose Block
2 Unit 1, 2 Unit 3
Make 60
Corner Block
1 Unit 1, 1 Unit 2,
2 Unit 4
Make 4
Edge 1 Block
1 Unit 1, 1 Unit 2,
1 Unit 3, 1 Unit 4
Make 16
Edge 2 Block
1 Unit 1, 1 Unit 2, 1
Unit 3, 1 Unit 4
Make 16

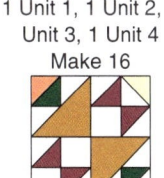

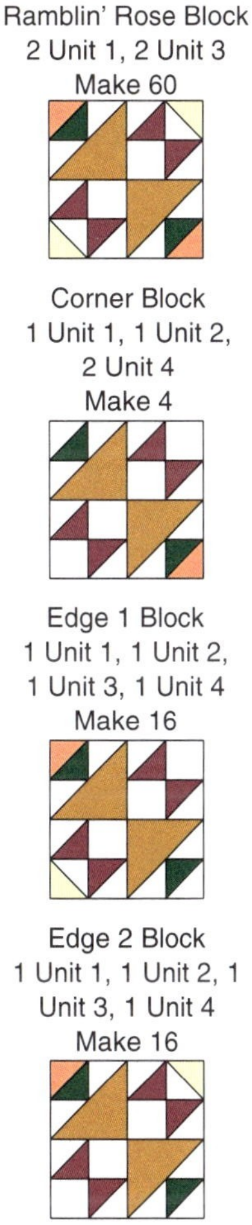

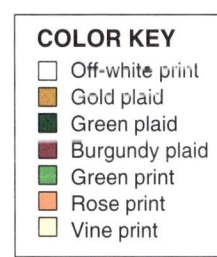

Figure 3
Combine block units to make blocks as shown.

CB	E1	E2	E1	E2	E1	E2	CB
E2							E1
E1							E2
E2							E1
E1							E2
E2							E1
E1							E2
E2							E1
E1							E2
E2							E1
E1							E2
CB	E2	E1	E2	E1	E2	E1	CB

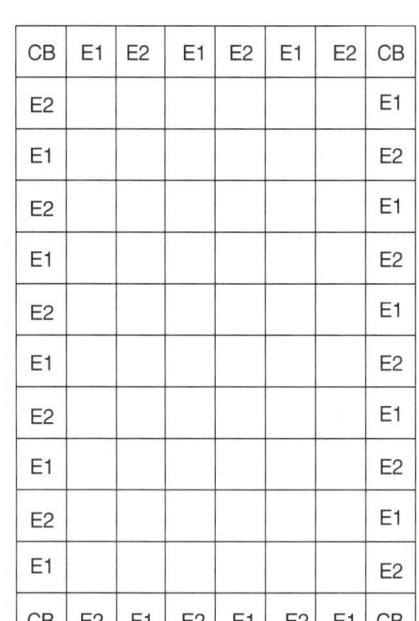

Figure 4
Arrange blocks in 12 rows of 8 blocks each, placing each block as shown.

CB—Corner Block
E1—Edge 1 Block
E2—Edge 2 Block
Unmarked blocks are Ramblin' Rose blocks.

COLOR KEY
- Off-white print
- Gold plaid
- Green plaid
- Burgundy plaid
- Green print
- Rose print
- Vine print

Corner Unit
Make 4
B-B Units
Make 180

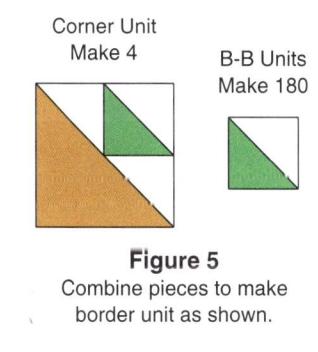

Figure 5
Combine pieces to make border unit as shown.

8. Sew a corner unit to each end of the 3½" x 48½" border strips cut in step 1 as shown in Figure 6; press. Sew these strips to the top and bottom of the pieced center; press seams toward strips.

3½" x 48½"

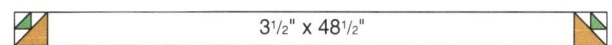

Figure 6
Sew a corner unit to each end of a 3½" x 48½" border strip as shown.

9. Join 19 B-B units as shown in Figure 7; repeat to make two 19-unit X border strips. Join 26 B-B units, as for 19-unit strips, to make two 26-unit X border strips.

Figure 7
Join B-B units to make X border strip as shown.

10. Join 19 B-B units as shown in Figure 8; repeat to make two 19-unit Y border strips. Join 26 B-B units, as for the 19-unit strips, to make two 26-unit Y border strips.

Figure 8
Join B-B units to make Y border strip as shown.

11. Join one 26-unit X border strip with one 26-unit Y border strip as shown in Figure 9; repeat. Sew the pieced strips to opposite long sides of the pieced top; press seams toward inner border strips.

12. Join one 19-unit X border strip with one 19-unit Y border strip, strip as in step 11; repeat. Sew the pieced strips to the top and bottom of the pieced top; press seams toward inner border strips.

13. Sandwich batting between quilt top and prepared backing piece; pin or baste layers to hold. Quilt as desired by hand or machine.

14. Bind edges with self-made or purchased binding to finish. ∎

Figure 9
Join X and Y border strips as shown.

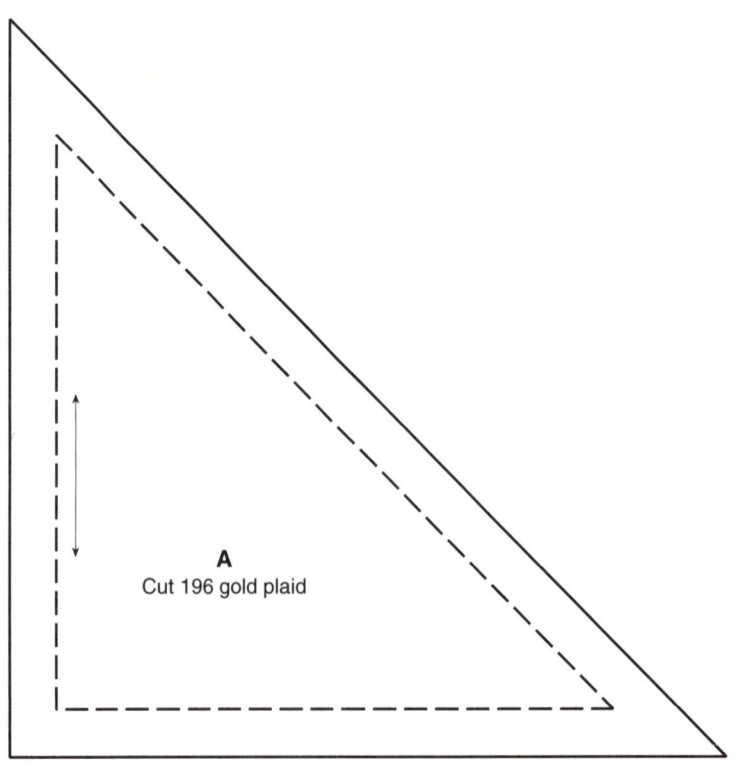

A
Cut 196 gold plaid

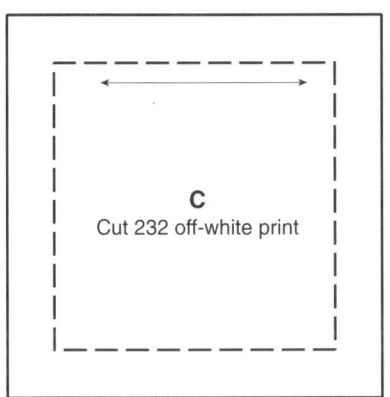

C
Cut 232 off-white print

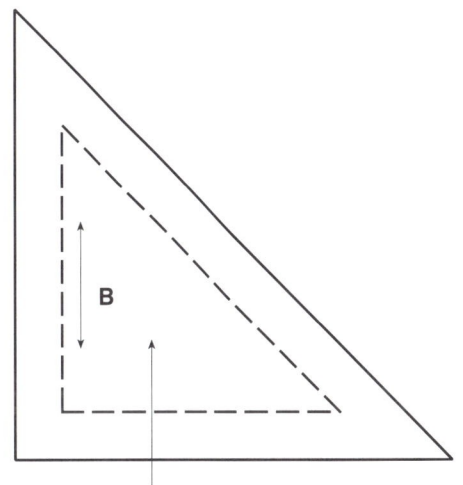

B

Cut 152 vine print, 156 rose print, 184 green print, 192 green plaid, 384 burgundy plaid & 1,148 off-white print

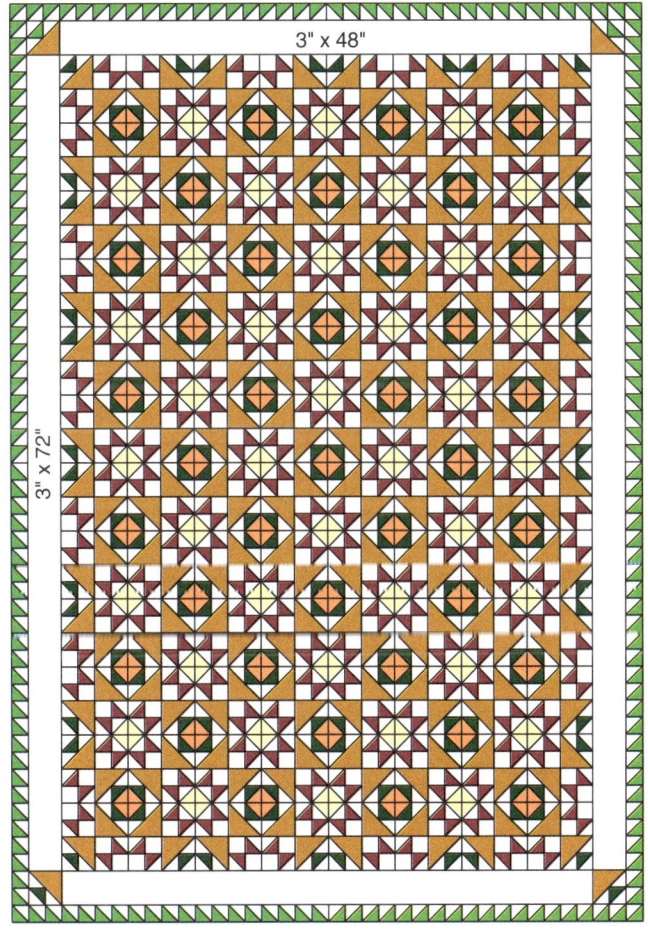

Ramblin' Rose
Placement Diagram
57" x 81"

HOUSE OF WHITE BIRCHES, BERNE, INDIANA 46711   WWW.WHITEBIRCHES.COM   Scrappy Garden Quilts   11

Flowers in Bloom

BY RUTH SWASEY

Simple circles cut from vintage reproduction prints create the flowers in this pretty quilt.

Project Specifications
Quilt Size: 84" x 98"
Block Size: 14" x 14"
Number of Blocks: 21

Fabric & Batting
- ⅙ yard green print
- ½ yard each 2 peach prints for pots
- ⅔ yard white print for binding
- 1 yard white print for H
- 1¼ yards total vintage reproduction print scraps for flowers
- 3¾ yards white stripe for G
- 4⅝ yards white solid for F
- Backing 90" x 104"
- Batting 90" x 104"

Tools & Supplies
- White all-purpose thread
- Clear nylon monofilament
- 30–35 used dryer sheets
- 9 yards fabric stabilizer
- Green machine-embroidery thread
- Basic sewing tools and supplies, water-erasable marker or pencil and 14" x 14" tracing paper

Making Blocks
1. Cut 21 squares 14½" x 14½" white solid for F; fold and crease to mark center.

Flowers in Bloom
14" x 14" Block

2. Transfer the entire block design to the 14" x 14" tracing paper.

3. Transfer the design to the F squares using a water-erasable marker or pencil, matching design center with crease marks on A squares.

4. Cut 21 squares fabric stabilizer 14" x 14"; center and pin a square behind each F square.

5. Using green machine-embroidery thread in the top of the machine and all-purpose thread in the bobbin, machine-stitch along stem lines using a

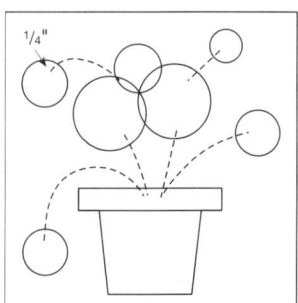

Figure 1
Extend stem stitching ¼" into appliqué spaces.

machine stem stitch, extending the stem lines into the appliqué areas ¼" as shown in Figure 1.

6. Prepare templates for appliqué shapes using patterns given. Cut as directed on each piece for one block, adding a ¼" seam allowance all around when cutting; repeat for 21 blocks.

7. Press the dryer sheets with a warm iron.

8. Pin several A, B or C shapes on each sheet with right side of fabric shape against the dryer sheet.

9. Sew all around pinned shapes using a ¼" seam allowance; cut out shapes.

10. Cut a slit in the dryer sheet side of each piece and turn right side out; press flat. *Note: Use a butter knife or something small with rounded end and run it around the seams to push into a perfect circle.*

11. Repeat steps 8–10 for all A, B and C pieces.

12. Turn under seam allowance on D and E except for top edge of E; press.

13. Place E on F matching marked lines; using clear nylon monofilament in the top of the machine and all-purpose thread in the bobbin and a machine blind-hem stitch, stitch E in place. Place D on top of E and stitch.

14. Arrange the A, B and C flower circles as marked on pattern; stitch in place as in step 13 to complete one block. Repeat for 21 blocks.

15. Remove fabric stabilizer.

Completing the Top

1. Cut 18 squares white stripe 14½" x 14½" for G and six 7½" x 14½" rectangles white print for H.

2. Join three appliquéd blocks with three G squares to make a row referring to Figure 2; repeat for four rows. Press seams toward G.

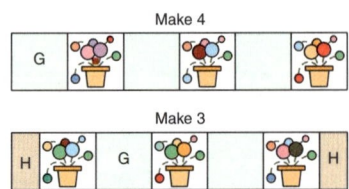

Figure 2
Join appliqué blocks with G squares and H rectangles to make rows.

3. Join two H rectangles with three appliquéd blocks and two G squares to make a row, again referring to Figure 2; repeat for three rows. Press seams toward G and H.

4. Arrange rows referring to the Placement Diagram; join rows to complete the pieced top. Press seams in one direction.

Finishing the Quilt

1. Sandwich batting between the completed top and prepared backing piece; pin or baste layers together to hold flat for quilting.

2. Quilt as desired by hand or machine. *Note: The sample shown was machine-quilted in a meandering floral design using clear nylon monofilament in the top of the machine and all-purpose thread in the bobbin.*

3. When quilting is complete, trim batting and backing even with quilted top; remove pins or basting.

4. Cut nine 2¼" by fabric width strips white print. Join strips on short ends to make one long strip for binding.

5. Fold the binding strip in half along length with wrong sides together; press.

6. Sew binding strip to quilt edge with raw edges matching, mitering corners and overlapping beginning and end; turn to backside. Hand- or machine-stitch in place. ■

Flowers In Bloom
Placement Diagram
84" x 98"

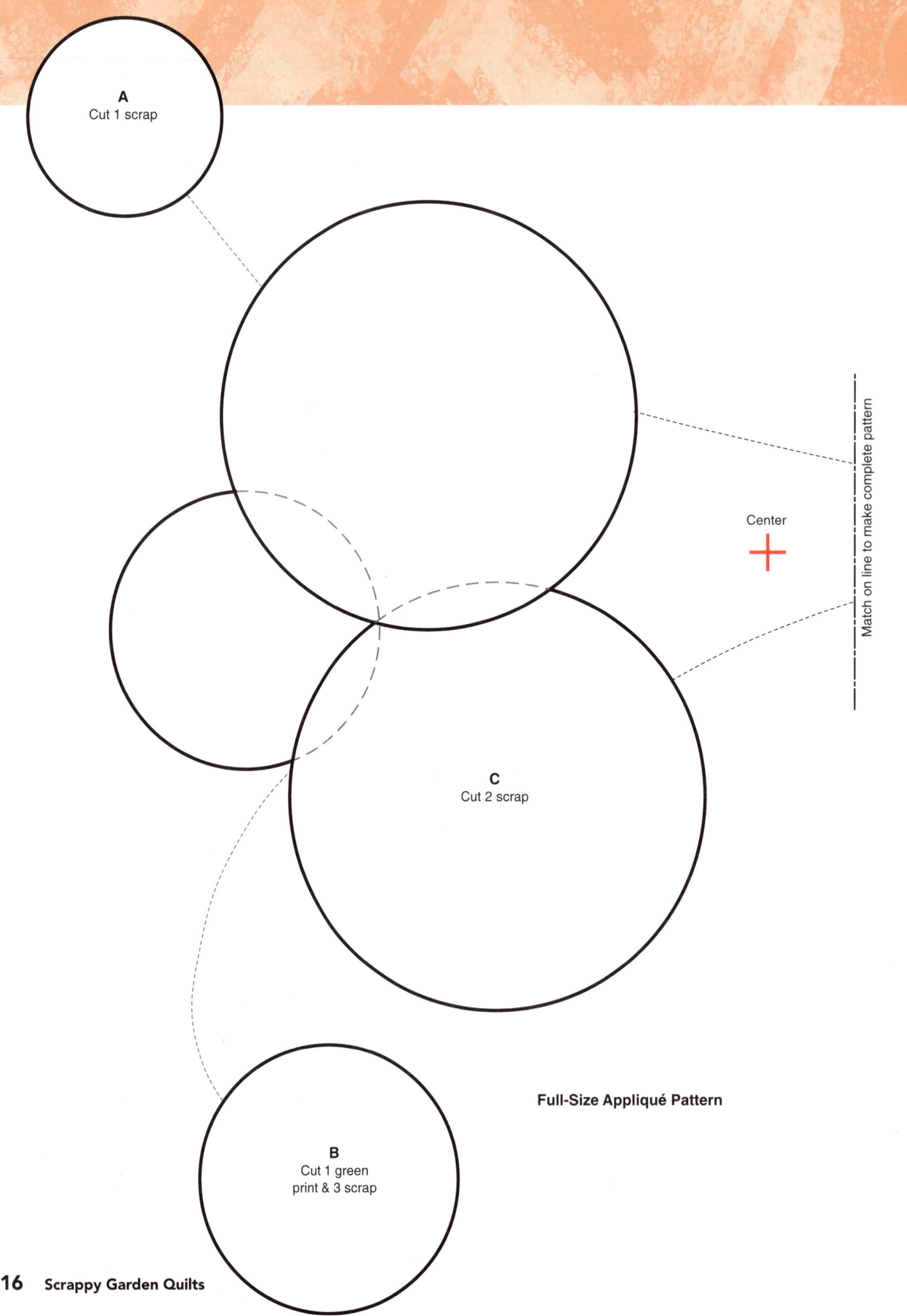

Full-Size Appliqué Pattern

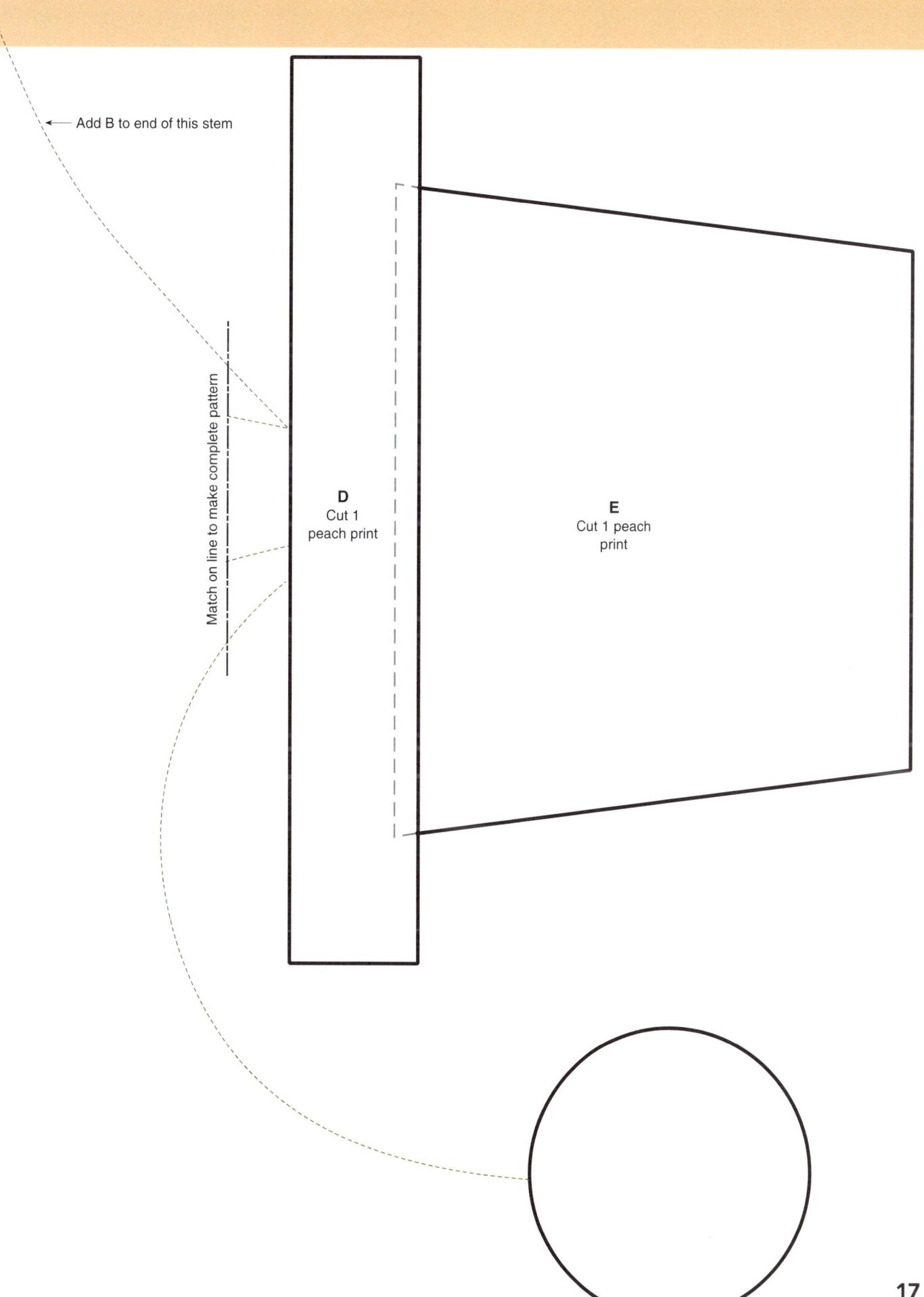

Blooming Cabins

BY RUTH SWASEY

Courthouse Steps blocks arranged in an alternating setting by rows create an unusual look in this large quilt.

Project Specifications
Quilt Size: 108" x 108"
Block Size: 13½" x 13½"
Number of Blocks: 40

Materials
- ½ yard light blue floral (piece 1)
- ½ yard cream print (pieces 2 and 3)
- ¾ yard multicolor floral for binding
- ⅞ yard pink tone-on-tone (pieces 6 and 7)
- ⅞ yard black tone-on-tone (pieces 16 and 17)
- ⅞ yard black/gray print (pieces 16 and 17)
- 1⅛ yards black rose print (pieces 8 and 9)
- 1⅛ yards pink print (pieces 10 and 11)
- 1¼ yards allover floral (pieces 14, 15 and C borders)
- 1¼ yards white floral (B borders)
- 1¾ yards black floral (pieces 4 and 5 and A borders)
- 2¼ yards black print (pieces 12 and 13 and D borders)
- Backing 114" x 114"
- Batting 114" x 114"

Tools & Supplies
- Neutral color all-purpose thread
- Quilting thread
- Basic sewing tools and supplies

Courthouse Steps A
13½" x 13½" Block

Courthouse Steps B
13½" x 13½" Block

Instructions
Completing Blocks

1. Cut and piece four 4¼" x 81½" strips black floral for A border strips; set aside.

2. Cut and piece four 1¾" x 81½" strips allover floral for C border strips; set aside.

3. Cut and piece four 4½" x 81½" strips black print for D border strips; set aside.

4. Cut four strips light blue floral 4" by fabric width.

5. Cut eight strips cream print 1¾" by fabric width.

6. Sew a light blue floral strip between two cream print strips with right sides together along length; press seams toward light blue floral strip. Repeat for four strip sets.

Scrappy Garden Quilts HOUSE OF WHITE BIRCHES, BERNE, INDIANA 46711 WWW.WHITEBIRCHES.COM

BLOOMING CABINS

7. Subcut strip sets into 4" segments to complete a 3-1-2 segment as shown in Figure 1; you will need 40 segments for block centers.

Figure 1
Subcut strip set into 4" segments.

8. Cut all remaining fabrics into 1¾" by fabric width strips except for white floral and multicolor floral. Label each fabric with piece numbers as indicated on the list of materials.

9. Referring to Figure 2 for order of piecing and colors, sew strips to the pieced center unit, pressing and trimming strips even with previously pieced units as shown in Figure 3 to complete 20 A and 20 B blocks. **Note:** *The only difference between A and B blocks is the last black strip. The A block uses the black tone-on-tone strips and the B block uses the black/gray print. This difference does show up on the quilt when the blocks are joined.* When blocks are finished, measure and trim to 14" x 14".

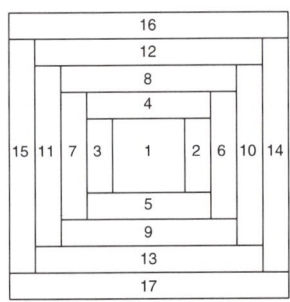

Figure 2
Make A and B blocks, sewing strips in numerical order referring to numbers assigned to fabrics for fabric order.

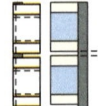

Figure 3
Sew press and trim as shown.

Completing the Top

1. Join three each A and B blocks, alternating blocks to make a row as shown in Figure 4; repeat for three rows. Press seams in one direction.

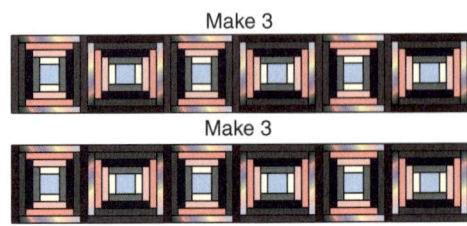

Figure 4
Join blocks, alternating A and B blocks to make rows.

2. Join three each A and B blocks, alternating blocks to make a row, again referring to Figure 4; repeat for three rows. Press seams in one direction.

3. Join the rows, alternating positioning of rows referring to the Placement Diagram; press seams in one direction.

4. Cut and piece eight 2¾" x 81½" B strips white floral.

5. Sew an A strip to a B strip to a C strip to a B strip to a D strip with right sides together along length to make a border strip referring to Figure 5; repeat for four border strips. Press seams toward darker fabrics.

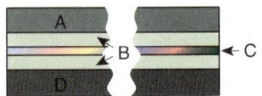

Figure 5
Sew an A strip to a B strip to a C strip to a B strip to a D strip.

6. Sew a border strip to two opposite sides of the pieced center; press seams toward strips.

7. Sew an A block to one end and a B block to the opposite end of each remaining border strip referring to Figure 6; press seams toward border strips.

8. Sew a strip to the remaining sides of the pieced center referring to the Placement Diagram for positioning of A and B blocks at corners; press seams toward strips.

Finishing the Quilt

Note: *The sample quilt was allover machine-quilted in patterned design.*

1. Prepare quilt top for quilting and quilt.

2. When quilting is complete, trim batting and backing edges even with the quilted top.

3. Prepare 12¼ yards multicolor floral binding and bind edges to finish.

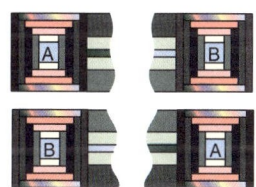

Figure 6
Sew an A block
to 1 end and a B block
to the opposite end of a border strip.

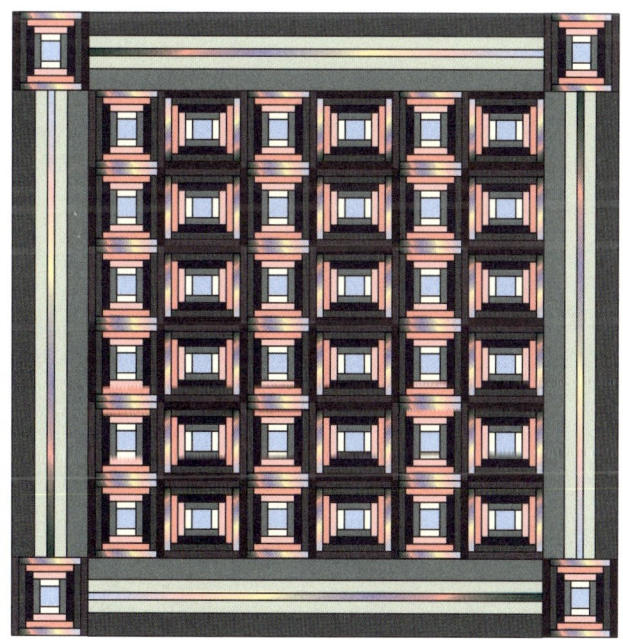

Blooming Cabins
Placement Diagram 108" x 108"

Home in the Garden

BY CHRISTINE SCHULTZ

This small wall quilt features simple piecing and appliqué. It's a perfect showcase for scraps of favorite fabrics and old buttons.

Project Specifications
Wall Quilt Size: 10½" x 21"

Fabric & Batting
- ⅛ yard each red check and background
- ¼ yard each blue and green prints
- ⅓ yard border fabric
- 1 fat quarter dark brown print
- Scraps for flowers and entrance
- Backing 13" x 24"
- Batting 13" x 24"
- 2 yards self-made or purchased binding

Tools & Supplies
- All-purpose thread to match fabrics
- 1 spool white quilting thread
- Tracing paper
- Freezer paper
- 4 buttons of different sizes and colors
- Basic sewing supplies and tools and tweezers

Instructions

1. Cut one strip each 1½" x 18" blue print and red check. Join strips along length. Cut apart to make two 1½" x 9" segments. Join these segments along length to make a pieced strip as shown in Figure 1.

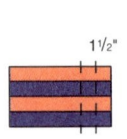

Figure 1
Join strip sets as shown.

2. Cut strip apart in 1½" segments as shown in Figure 2. Join five segments as shown in Figure 3 to make the birdhouse base.

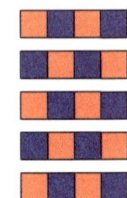

Figure 2
Cut strip apart in 1½" segments.

Figure 3
Join 5 segments as shown.

3. Cut an A triangle from red check. Sew the triangle to one short end of the birdhouse base as shown in Figure 4.

4. Cut two strips background fabric 1¼" x 6". Sew one of these strips to two opposite sides of the birdhouse base; place a straightedge ruler on the edge of the top triangle and trim strips at the same angle as shown in Figure 5.

Figure 4
Sew A to 1 short side of pieced birdhouse base.

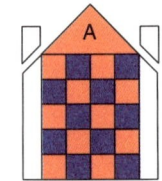

Figure 5
Trim strips even with edge of A.

HOME IN THE GARDEN

5. Cut two strips brown print 1¼" x 6". Sew a strip to the left side of A as shown in Figure 6; press seam toward strip. Repeat for right side. Trim strips even with side piece as shown in Figure 7.

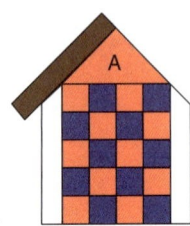

Figure 6
Sew a strip to the left side of A.

Figure 7
Trim even with side strips.

6. Cut two A triangles from background fabric. Sew a triangle to each side of the birdhouse section to complete as shown in Figure 8. Cut hole piece; appliqué in the center of birdhouse referring to the Placement Diagram and photo of project for positioning.

Figure 8
Sew A triangles to top of pieced section.

7. Cut one strip brown print 1½" x 8½". Cut two strips background 2¾" x 8½". Sew the brown strip between the two background strips.

8. Sew the brown/background section to the bottom of the birdhouse section.

9. Cut two strips blue print 1" x 16½"; sew a strip to opposite long sides of the pieced center. Press seams toward strips.

10. Cut two strips blue print 1" x 7"; sew a strip to top and bottom of the pieced center. Press seams toward strips.

11. Cut two strips border fabric 2½" x 17½"; sew a strip to opposite long sides of the pieced center. Press seams toward strips.

12. Cut two strips border fabric 2½" x 11"; sew a strip to top and bottom of pieced center. Press seams toward strips.

13. Draw a full-size pattern for appliqué onto tracing paper. Transfer pattern to bottom half of pieced center using a water-erasable marker or pencil.

14. Cut ½"-wide bias strips from green print to make an 18" piece. Press or baste in edges ⅛". Appliqué in place using drawing as a guide for placement of stems.

15. Cut finished-size pieces for each pattern shape from freezer paper. Iron freezer-paper shapes to the wrong side of the flower and leaf scraps as directed on each piece for color.

16. Cut out shapes leaving 3⁄16" turn-under allowance around each piece. Pin the pieces in place on background using traced lines as guides for placement.

17. Using matching thread and a needle to help turn edges over paper shapes, appliqué pieces in place, layering as necessary to complete the design.

18. When appliqué is complete, carefully slit behind pieces from the backside; remove freezer paper using tweezers, if necessary. Press piece from right side.

19. Sandwich batting between bordered top and prepared backing piece; pin or baste layers together to hold. Quilt as desired by hand or machine.

20. Bind edges with self-made or purchased binding.

21. Sew a button in the center of each flower after binding and quilting are complete. ∎

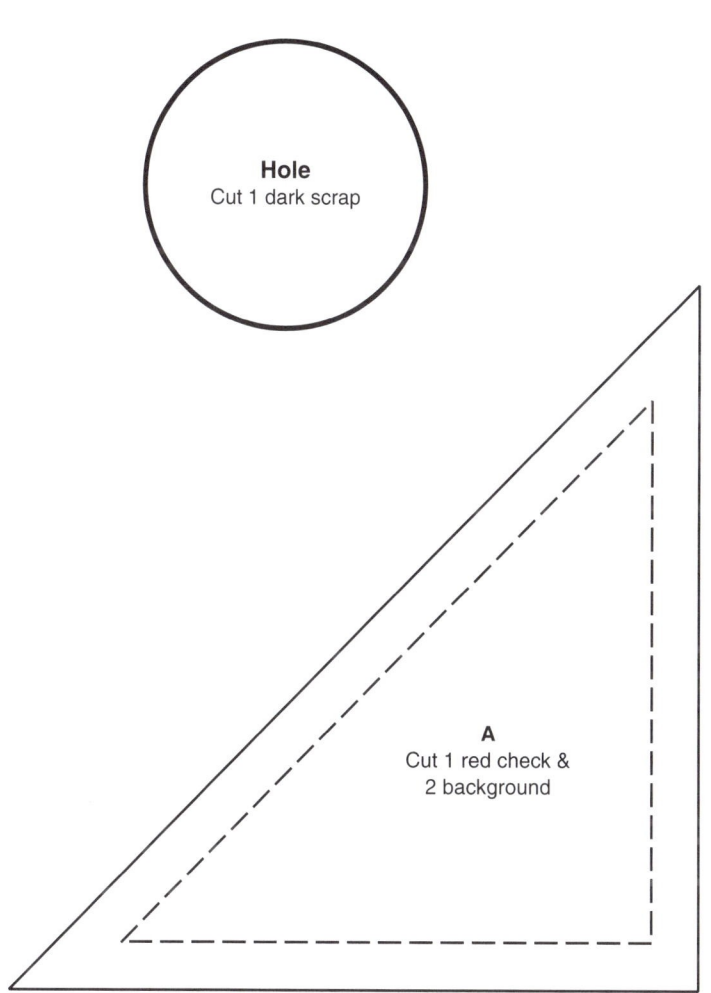

Hole
Cut 1 dark scrap

A
Cut 1 red check &
2 background

Home in the Garden
Placement Diagram
10½" x 21" Block

HOUSE OF WHITE BIRCHES, BERNE, INDIANA 46711   WWW.WHITEBIRCHES.COM   **Scrappy Garden Quilts** 25

HOME IN THE GARDEN

Full-Size Appliqué Pattern

X indicates button placement

26 Scrappy Garden Quilts HOUSE OF WHITE BIRCHES, BERNE, INDIANA 46711

Coming Up Roses

BY JILL REBER

Every garden should have a bed of roses.

Project Specifications
Wall Quilt Size: 28" x 34"
Block Size: 6" x 6"
Number of Blocks: 12

Fabric & Batting
- ¼ yard each 3 different rose prints for flowers
- ½ yard dark green solid for stems and binding
- ⅓ yard green print for leaves
- ¾ yard light print for background
- ¾ yard floral print for outside borders
- Backing 32" x 38"
- Batting 32" x 38"
- 4¼ yards self-made or purchased binding

Tools & Supplies
- 1 spool each off-white, rose and dark green quilting thread
- Neutral color all-purpose thread
- Basic sewing supplies and tools and Master Piece 45 ruler

Project Notes
The Master Piece 45 ruler was used to construct the project shown. You may purchase this ruler at your local quilt shop, use templates given or cut using strip-method instructions given.

Traditional Method
1. Prepare templates using pattern pieces given. Cut as directed on each piece. *Note: Follow directions given in the package for using Master*

Coming up Roses
6" x 6" Block

Piece 45 ruler, if you choose to use it rather than templates or strip-cutting methods.

2. Referring to Figure 1 to piece one block, sew a rose print B to a background C to a green print B; repeat reversing placement of B colors. Sew a rose print A to a green print A. Sew a background D to each long side of E; sew to a green print A. Sew a background A to the rose end of one B-C-B unit. Arrange pieced units and join to complete one block; repeat for 12 blocks. Press all blocks.

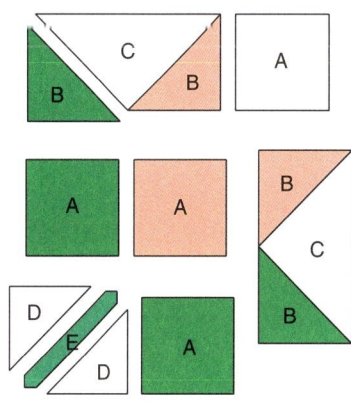

Figure 1
Join units to complete 1 block.

3. Arrange the blocks in four rows of three blocks each. Join blocks in rows; join rows. Press pieced center.

4. Cut two strips background 1½" x 18½"; sew to top and bottom. Cut two strips background 1½" x 26½"; sew to opposite long sides. Press seams toward border strips.

5. To piece corner blocks, sew a background B to a rose print B; repeat. Sew rose print side of one unit to a rose print A. Sew rose print side of one unit to a background A. Join these two units as shown in Figure 2 to complete one corner block; press. Repeat for four blocks.

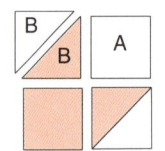

Figure 2
Join units to complete corner block.

6. Cut two strips floral print 4½" x 20½"; sew to top and bottom. Cut two strips floral print 4½" x 26½". Sew a corner square to each end of each strip referring to the Placement Diagram for positioning of blocks. Sew a strip to opposite long sides; press seams toward strips.

7. Sandwich batting between the completed top and prepared backing; pin or baste layers together to hold flat.

8. Quilt as desired by hand or machine using off-white quilting thread on background and borders, green quilting thread on green print pieces and rose quilting thread on rose print pieces. When quilting is complete, trim edges even. Bind edges with self-made or purchased binding to finish.

Quick Method

1. Cut one strip from each rose print 2⅞" by fabric width. Cut eight 2⅞" segments from each rose print strip. Trim remaining strips to 2½" wide. Cut four 2½" segments from two rose prints and eight from one rose print for A squares.

2. Cut each 2⅞" x 2⅞" square in half on one diagonal to make B triangles. *Note: You will have extra triangles of these colors.*

3. Cut one strip dark green solid 3½" x 10½". Cut strip into ⅞" x 3½" rectangles for E stem pieces, or use E templates; you will need 12 E pieces.

4. Cut one strip green print 2⅞" by fabric width. Cut strip into 2⅞" segments; repeat for 12 segments. Cut each segment in half on the diagonal to make 24 B triangles.

5. Cut two strips green print 2½" by fabric width. Cut into 2½" segments; repeat for 24 segments for A.

6. Cut two strips background 2⅝" by fabric width. Cut strips into 2⅝" segments; cut in half on one diagonal to make D triangles. Repeat for 24 triangles.

7. Cut four 2⅞" x 2⅞" squares background. Cut each square in half on one diagonal for B triangles.

8. Cut six squares background 5¼" x 5¼". Cut each square in half on both diagonals for C triangles.

9. Cut one strip background 2½" by fabric width. Cut into 2½" segments for A; you will need 16 A squares.

10. Join pieces as for Traditional Method referring to Figure 1 to complete blocks.

11. Piece corner blocks as for Traditional Method referring to Figure 2.

12. Complete project referring to Traditional Method steps 3–8 to complete project. ■

COMING UP ROSES

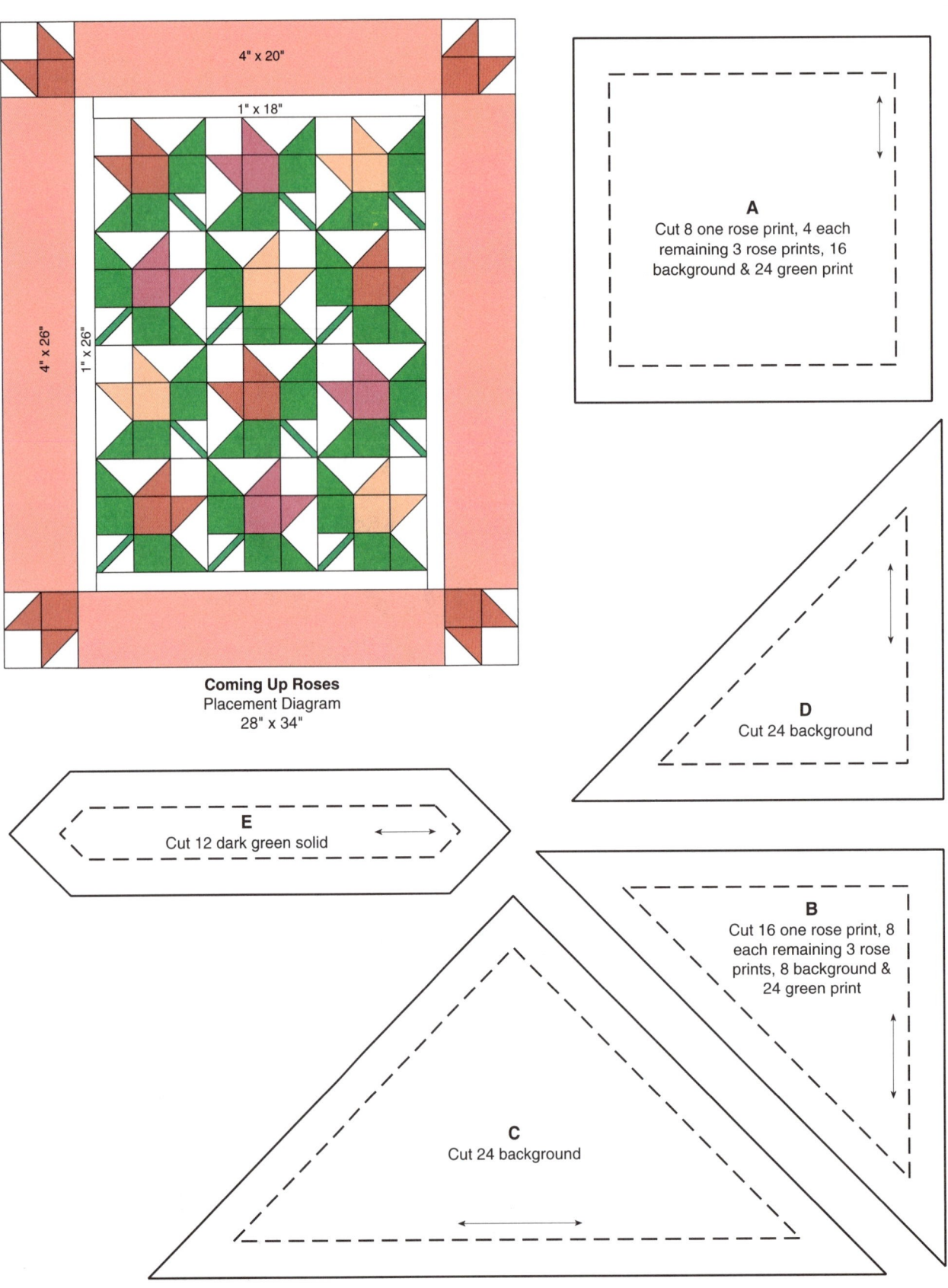

Coming Up Roses
Placement Diagram
28" x 34"

Star Flower

BY MARIAN SHENK

Use narrow bias strips to create petals around the star shapes to make these flowers really sparkle.

Project Specifications
Quilt Size 26¾" x 26¾"
Block size: 8" x 8"
Number of Blocks: 4

Fabric & Batting
- ¼ yard dark green print for stars and corners
- ¼ yard each green, gold and rose prints for corners
- ½ yard off-white print for background
- ½ yard pastel print for corners and bias
- 1 yard border stripe
- Batting 31" x 31"
- Backing 31" x 31"
- 3½ yards self-made or purchased binding

Tools & Supplies
- Coordinating all-purpose thread
- 1 spool off-white quilting thread
- Basic sewing supplies and tools

Instructions

1. Prepare templates using pattern pieces given. Cut as directed on each piece. Transfer bias placement line to H and HR pieces.

2. Sew H to HR, stopping and starting at seam allowance as shown in Figure 1.

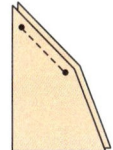

Figure 1
Sew H to HR, stopping and starting on seam line as shown.

3. Cut 1½"-wide bias strips from 16" x 16" square pastel print. Join strips on short ends to make a 5½-yard length of bias. Cut into 16 pieces 10" long. Fold each in half.

4. Pin raw edge on dotted line marked on H pattern; hand-stitch ¼" from edge through folded bias tape and H pieces as shown in Figure 2. After stitching, fold bias tape over raw edge to cover seam; hand-stitch in place on folded edge. Repeat for all H-HR units.

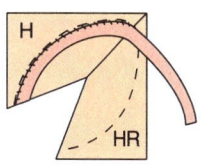

Figure 2
Place raw edge on dotted line; stitch ¼" away.

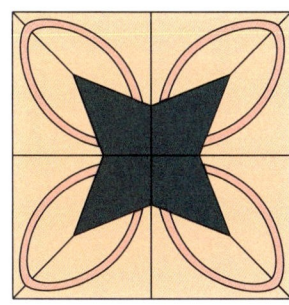

Star
8" x 8" Block

STAR FLOWER

5. Set piece G into H-HR units. Join four H-HR-G units as shown in Figure 3 to make a Star block; press. Repeat for four Star blocks.

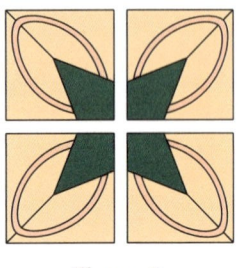

Figure 3
Join 4 units to make Star block.

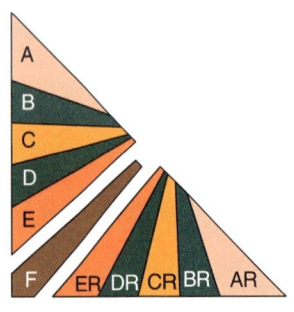

Figure 4
Join pieced units with F.

6. Sew A to B to C to D to E; repeat with reverse pieces. Press seams in one direction. Join two pieced units with F to complete one corner unit as shown in Figure 4; repeat for four corner units.

7. Sew the four Star blocks together in two rows of two blocks each; join rows to complete center unit. Press seams in one direction.

8. Sew a corner unit to each side of the center unit; press seams toward corner units.

9. Cut four strips border print 2½" x 28" (strips are cut longer than needed for mitering), cutting each strip from the same design on border print to make four strips exactly alike. Fold strips crosswise to mark center. Match center of strip to center of pieced quilt top; pin in place. Stitch, mitering corners; press seams toward strips.

10. Sandwich batting between bordered quilt and prepared backing piece; pin or baste to hold. Quilt as desired by hand or machine.

11. Bind edges with self-made or purchased bias binding to finish.

Star Flower
Placement Diagram
26¾" x 26¾"

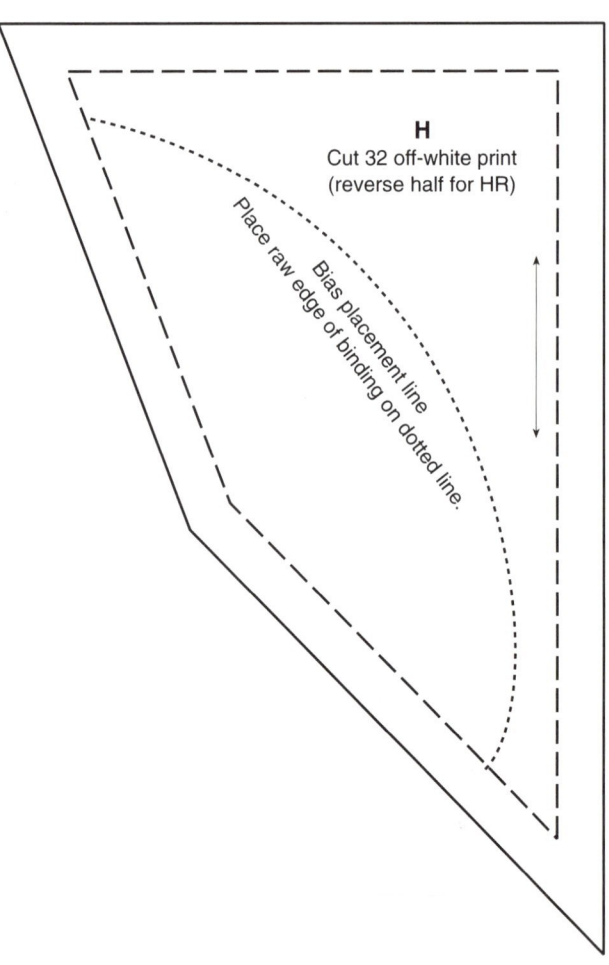

H
Cut 32 off-white print
(reverse half for HR)

STAR FLOWER

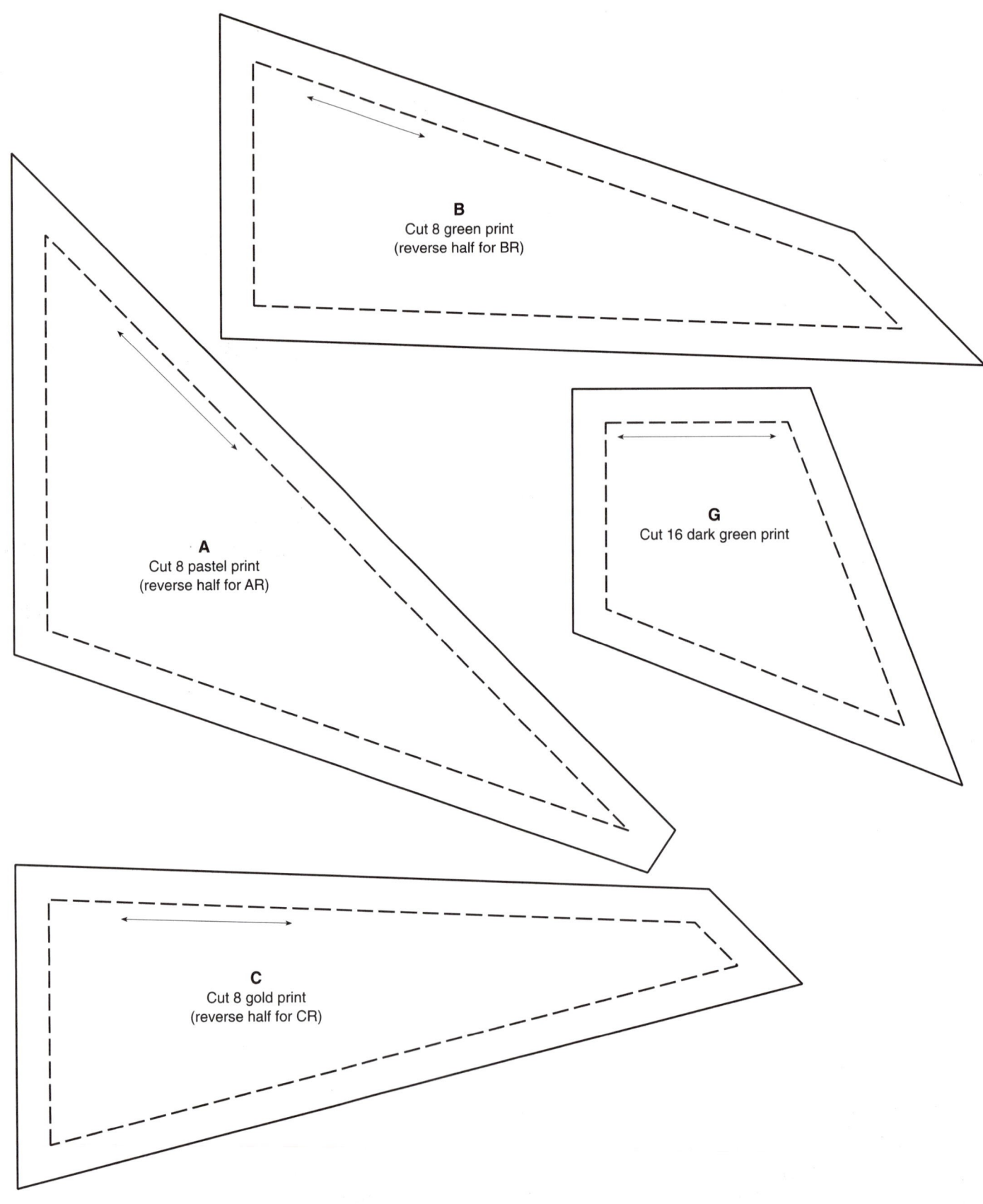

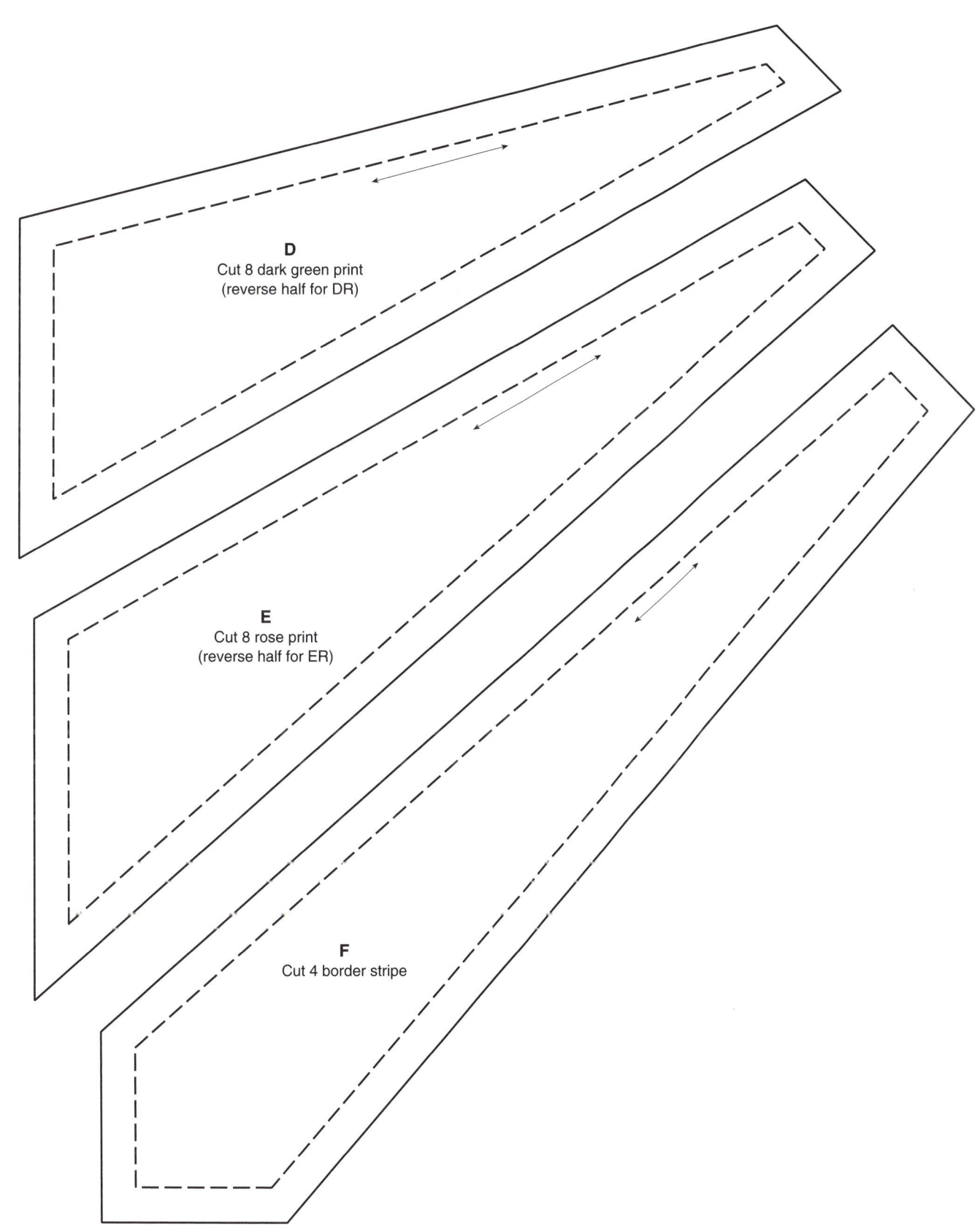

Flower Fun

BY LUCY FAZELY

Bright-colored 3-D flowers and butterflies make this little wall quilt the perfect accent to make any room sparkle.

Project Specifications
Quilt Size: 18" x 24"

Fabric & Batting
- 12½" x 18½" rectangle beige-on-beige print
- ⅛ yard yellow/blue stripe
- ¼ yard red print
- ¼ yard green print
- ⅓ yard yellow print
- Scraps bright prints
- 2" x 3" scrap blue
- Backing 22" x 28"
- Batting 22" x 28"
- 2½ yards self-made or purchased blue binding

Tools & Supplies
- 1 spool each beige, black and gold all-purpose thread
- Basic sewing tools and supplies

Making Background Quilt
1. Cut two strips green print 3½" x 12½"; sew a strip to each 12½" side of the 12½" x 18½" beige-on-beige print background piece. Cut two strips green print 3½" x 24½"; sew a strip to each long side of the pieced section. Press seams toward strips.

2. Sandwich batting between bordered top and prepared backing piece; pin or baste layers together to hold flat.

3. Machine-quilt in the ditch of border seams and in a freehand design on the center background using beige all-purpose thread. When quilting is complete, trim edges even; remove pins or basting.

4. Bind edges with self-made or purchased binding.

Daisies
1. Prepare template for daisy petal and center using pattern pieces given.

2. Make four yellow print daisies and two yellow/blue stripe daisies.

3. For each daisy, cut 16 pieces of fabric 1½" x 2½". Lay two pieces with right sides together. Trace daisy petal template on top; stitch around curved lines, leaving straight end open as shown in Figure 1. Trim seams to ⅛". Cut short flat side even with traced line referring to Figure 2. Turn right side out; press. Repeat for eight petals.

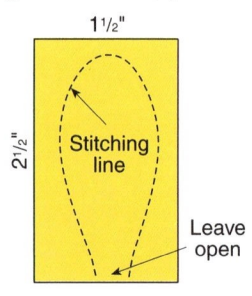

Figure 1
Stitch around curved edges; leave straight edge open.

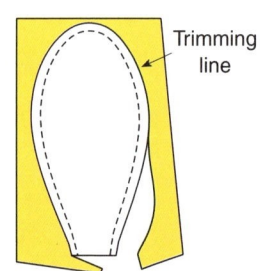

Figure 2
Trim to make a ⅛" seam on curved edges; trim even with straight line.

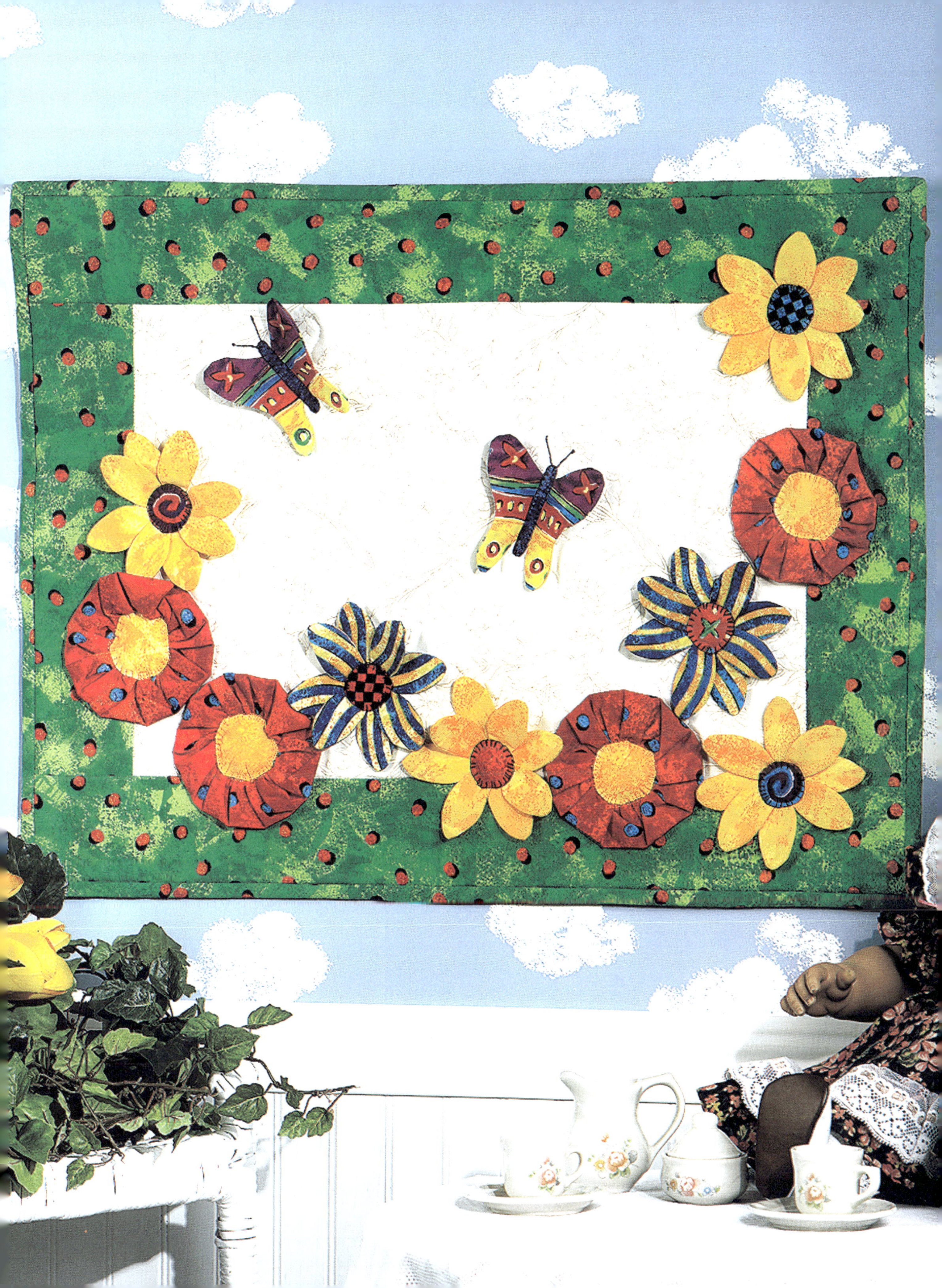

FLOWER FUN

4. Make four petal sets by sewing two open ends together. Layer the petal sets on top of each other as shown in Figure 3 to make a flower; baste together. Repeat for six daisies.

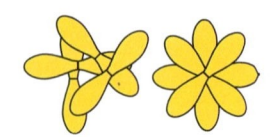

Figure 3
Layer petal sets to make a flower.

5. To make one daisy center, cut two 1½" x 1½" squares bright print. Lay pieces right sides together; trace daisy center shape on top piece. Sew all around circle. Trim seam allowance to ⅛". On back side, cut an X in the fabric, being careful not to cut through to top layer. Turn right side out through X. Press and pin over center of daisy. Repeat to make six daisy centers. Set aside.

Yo-Yo Flowers

1. Cut four 8"-diameter circles red print. Cut four 3½"-diameter circles yellow print. Baste a line of stitching ⅛" around edge of all circles, knotting the end of the thread. Pull the thread end on each circle to gather and make a yo-yo.

2. Lay the raw edges of a yellow print yo-yo facing the raw edges of a red print yo-yo; pin together. Set aside.

Butterflies

1. Prepare template for butterfly shapes. For each butterfly, cut four pieces bright print 2½" x 4". Lay two pieces right sides together. Trace butterfly wing shape on one set; reverse template and trace on second set.

2. Stitch along marked lines except on straight edge; trim seam to ⅛". Cut along marked line on long straight edge; turn right side out. Butt the two wings together along raw edges; baste.

3. Trace butterfly body onto 2" x 3" scrap blue. Stitch on traced line, leaving 1" open along one edge. Trim seam allowance to ⅛"; turn right side out. Hand-stitch opening closed. Press; pin over butterfly wings covering raw edges. Repeat for second butterfly. Set aside.

Finishing

1. Lay the flowers and butterflies on quilt referring to the Placement Diagram and photo of quilt for positioning suggestions.

2. Using black all-purpose thread and a machine overcast stitch, secure the edges of butterfly bodies and daisy centers to the background. Satin-stitch antennae on each butterfly.

3. Using gold all-purpose thread and a machine overcast stitch, secure the edges of the yellow print yo-yo flower centers. *Note: The yo-yo centers will not always be smooth circles and may have some straight edges.*

4. Prepare a sleeve for hanging if desired. ■

Daisy Center

Leave open for turning

Daisy Petal

Butterfly Body

Leave open for turning

Butterfly Wing
(reverse 1)

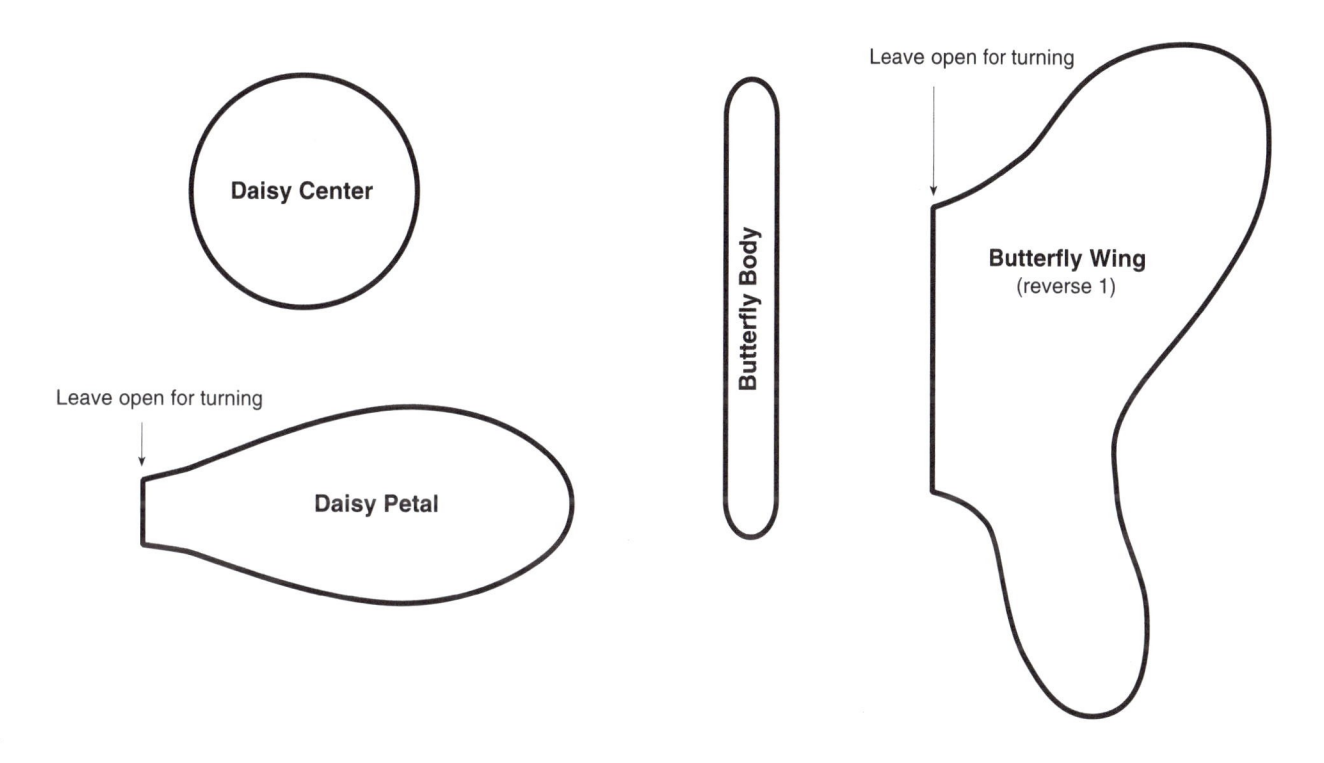

3" x 24"

3" x 12"

Flower Fun
Placement Diagram
18" x 24"

HOUSE OF WHITE BIRCHES, BERNE, INDIANA 46711　　WWW.WHITEBIRCHES.COM　　Scrappy Garden Quilts　　39

Rainbow Butterflies

BY RUTH SWASEY

Pieced butterfly motifs in a rainbow of colors fly across this colorful quilt.

Project Specifications
Quilt Size: 40" x 49½"
Block Size: 10" x 10"
Number of Blocks: 12

Fabric & Batting
- Scraps bright prints to total 1 yard
- ¼ yard green print
- ½ yard pink print for binding
- 1 yard white-on-white print
- 1 yard white print
- Batting 46" x 56"
- Backing 46" x 56"

Tools & Supplies
- Neutral color all-purpose thread
- Pink and green machine-embroidery thread
- White machine-quilting thread
- 6 packages variegated jumbo rickrack
- 2 yards fusible web
- Freezer paper
- Black permanent fabric pen
- Basic sewing tools and supplies

Making Butterfly Blocks
1. Trace the butterfly motifs onto freezer paper to make 12 copies each.

2. Cut bright print scrap fabric patches at least ¼" larger than each piece from A to G.

Rainbow Butterfly
10" x 10" Block

3. Pin the A piece right side up on the A space on the unmarked side of one freezer-paper section; pin B to A as shown in Figure 1.

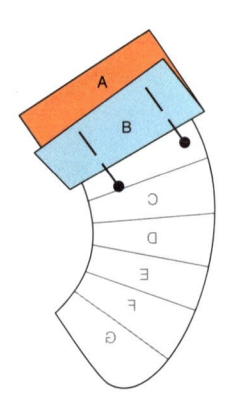

Figure 1
Pin the A piece right side up on the A space on the unmarked side of 1 freezer-paper section; pin B to A.

4. Turn paper over and stitch on the marked line between the A and B pieces as shown in Figure 2.

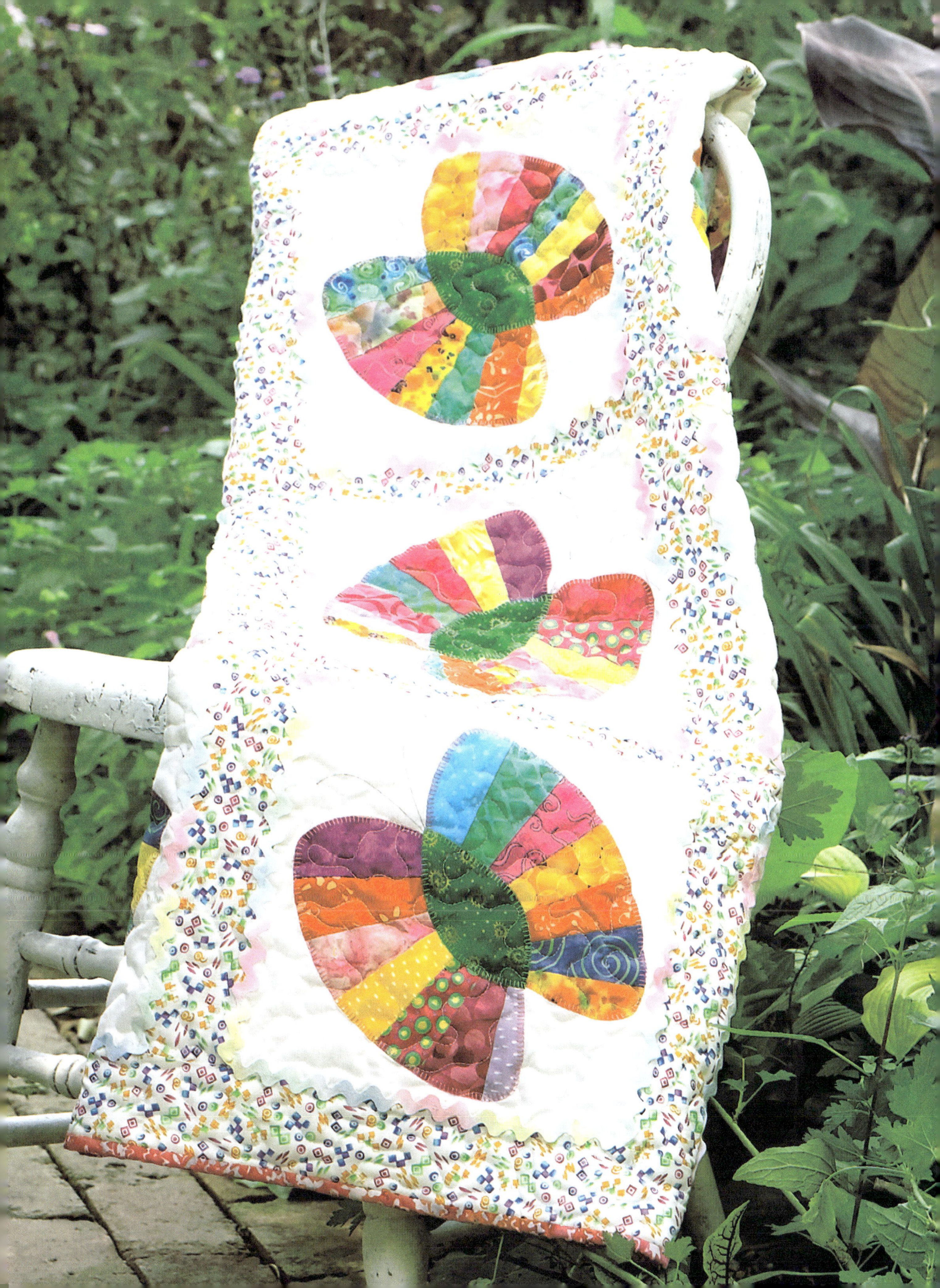

RAINBOW BUTTERFLIES

Turn paper over again and press B to the right side as shown in Figure 3; continue adding pieces in alphabetical order until the freezer paper is covered.

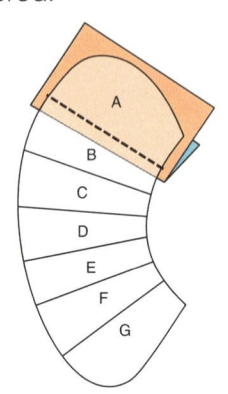

Figure 2
Stitch on the marked line between the A and B pieces.

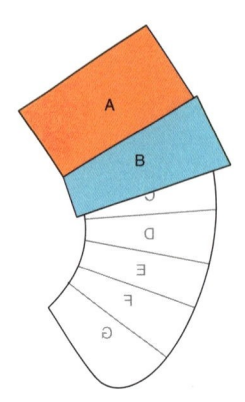

Figure 3
Turn paper over again and press B to the right side.

5. Trim freezer paper along outside cutting line as shown in Figure 4 to complete one wing unit. Repeat for 12 and 12 reverse wing units.

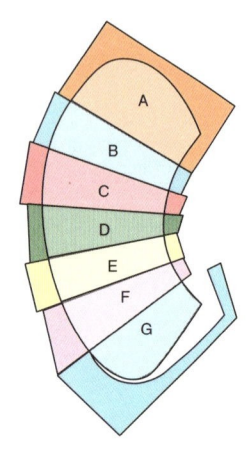

Figure 4
Trim freezer paper along outside cutting line.

6. Remove paper from each piece.

7. Trace 12 and 12 reverse wings onto the paper side of the fusible web. Cut out on marked line. Fuse one shape to the wrong side of each wing unit; remove paper backing.

8. Cut 12 squares white-on-white print 10½" x 10½"; press and crease to mark diagonal centers.

9. Using the diagonal center crease as a guide, pin one wing and one reverse wing to each background square; when satisfied with positioning, fuse shapes in place.

10. Trace 12 body pieces onto the fusible transfer web; fuse to the wrong side of the green print. Cut out shapes on traced lines; remove paper backing.

11. Position a body shape between wing shapes on fused blocks; fuse in place. **Note:** *Body should overlap wings to hide raw edges.*

12. Using green machine-embroidery thread and a machine buttonhole stitch, stitch around each body shape. Repeat with pink machine-embroidery thread around each wing.

13. Transfer antennae pattern to each block using pattern given and black permanent fabric pen to complete blocks.

Quilt Top Construction

1. Cut nine 2" x 10½" strips white print for H.

2. Join four blocks and three H strips to make a vertical row as shown in Figure 5; press seams toward H. Repeat for three rows referring to the Placement Diagram for positioning of butterflies.

3. Cut and piece four strips each 3" x 45" white print for J strips. Join the block rows with the J strips; press seams toward strips.

Figure 5
Join 4 blocks and 3 H strips to make a vertical row.

42 SCRAPPY GARDEN QUILTS HOUSE OF WHITE BIRCHES, BERNE, INDIANA 46711 WWW.WHITEBIRCHES.COM

4. Cut two 3" x 40½" strips white print for K strips; sew a K strip to the top and bottom of the pieced section to complete the quilt top; press seams toward strips.

5. Cover each seam around blocks with variegated jumbo rickrack and stitch in place through the center of the rickrack using white machine-quilting thread, folding under end and overlapping beginning end.

Finishing the Quilt

1. Sandwich batting between the completed top and prepared backing piece; pin or baste layers together to hold flat for quilting.

2. Quilt as desired by hand or machine. *Note: The quilt shown was machine-quilted in a meandering design using white machine-quilting thread.*

3. When quilting is complete, trim batting and backing even with quilted top; remove pins or basting.

4. Cut five 2¼" by fabric width strips pink print. Join strips on short ends to make one long strip for binding.

5. Fold the binding strip in half along length with wrong sides together; press.

6. Sew binding strip to quilt edge with raw edges matching, mitering corners and overlapping beginning and end; turn to the backside. Hand- or machine-stitch in place. ■

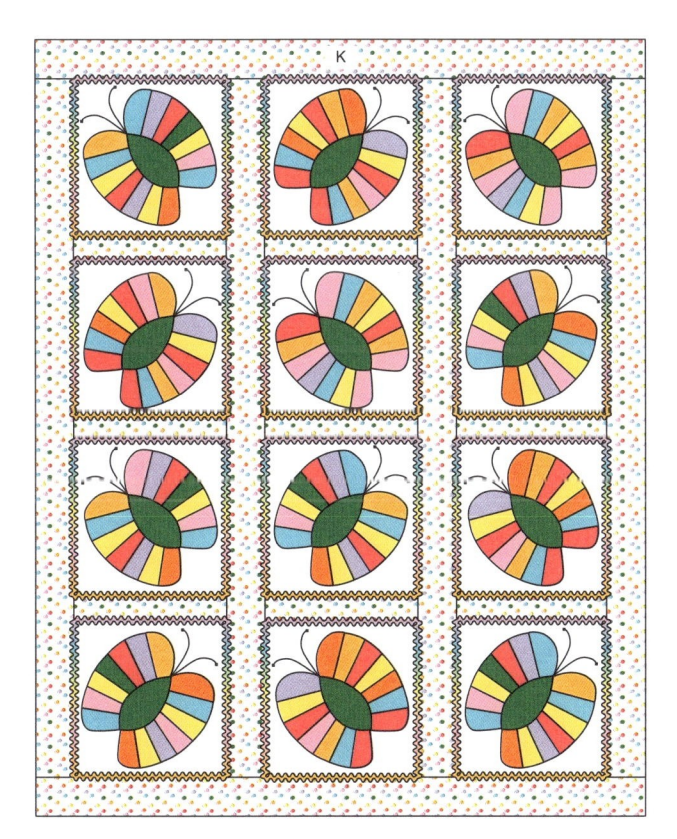

Rainbow Butterflies
Placement Diagram
40" x 49½"

RAINBOW BUTTERFLIES

AR

BR

CR

DR

ER

FR

GR

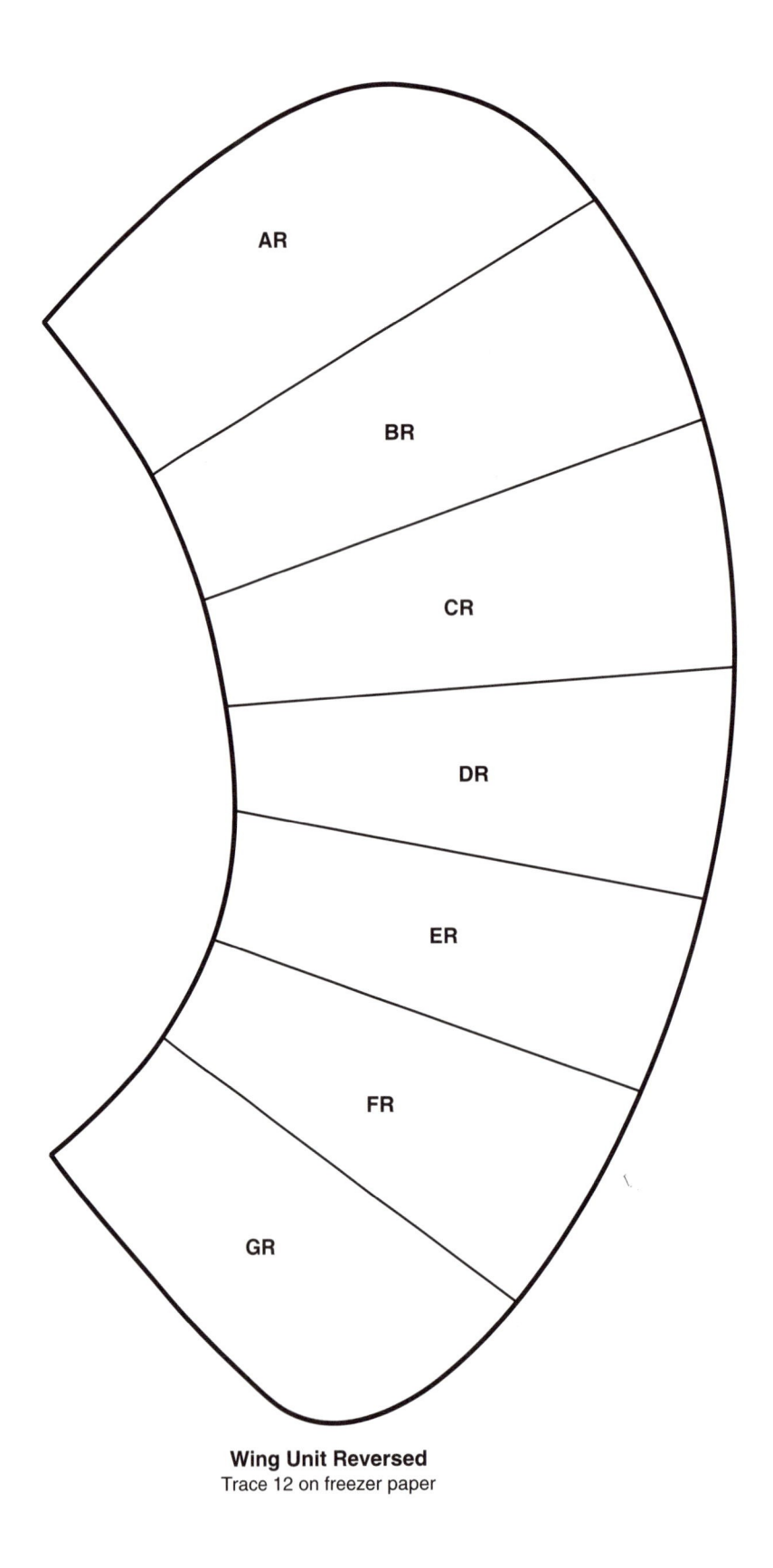

Wing Unit Reversed
Trace 12 on freezer paper

A

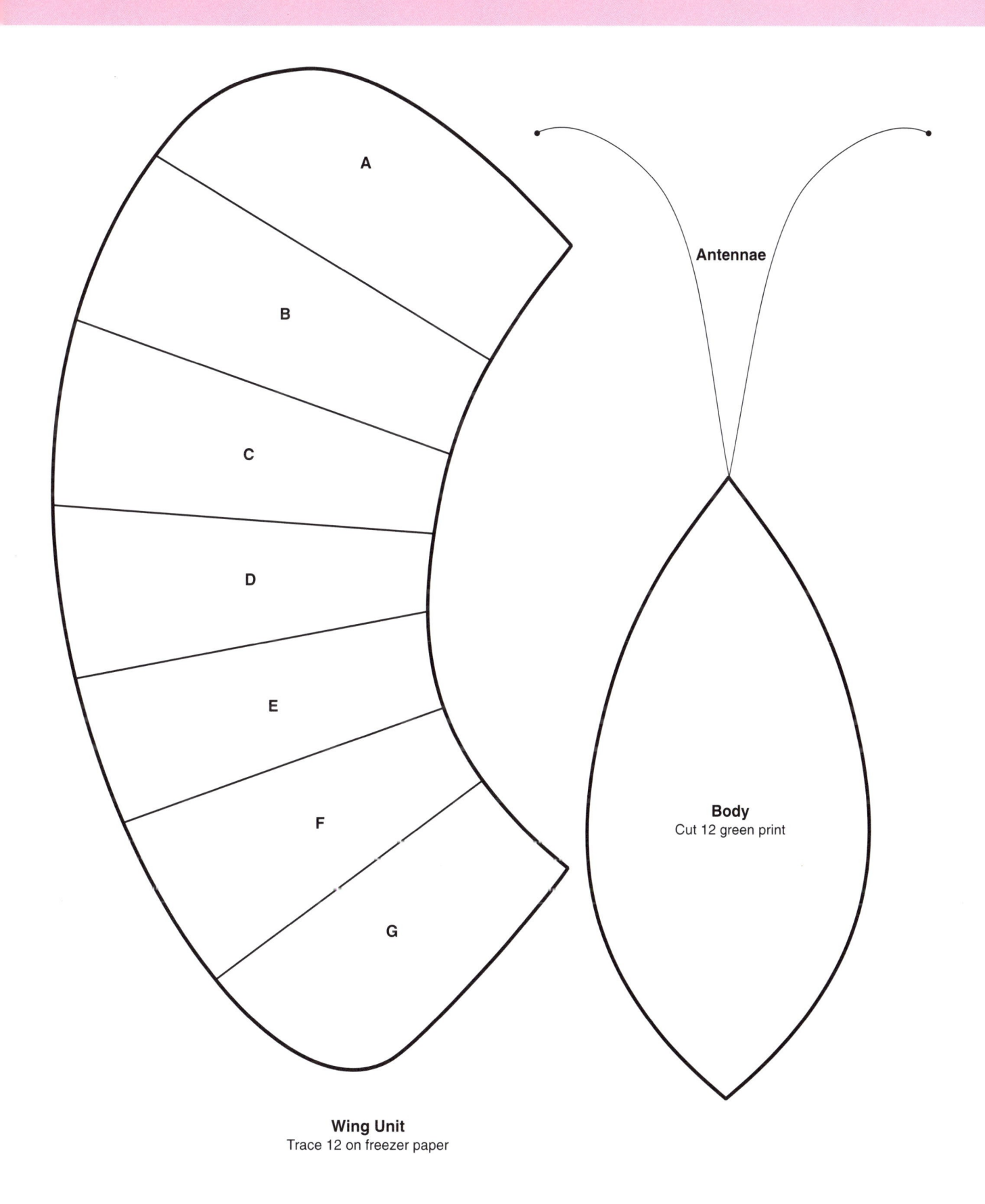

B

C

D

E

F

G

Antennae

Body
Cut 12 green print

Wing Unit
Trace 12 on freezer paper

HOUSE OF WHITE BIRCHES, BERNE, INDIANA 46711   WWW.WHITEBIRCHES.COM   **Scrappy Garden Quilts** 45

My Garden Path

BY JULIE WEAVER

Appliquéd flowers peek over the top of the pieced fabric fences in this pretty wall quilt.

Project Specifications
Quilt Size: 40" x 58"
Block Size: 10" x 16"
Number of Blocks: 9

Fabric & Batting
- 1 fat quarter each 2 blue prints
- 1 fat quarter each 3 pink, 3 purple and 3 red prints for flowers
- 1 fat quarter each 2 green and 2 yellow prints for stems, leaves and flower centers
- 1 yard medium green print
- 1⅓ yards white-on-white print
- Batting 46" x 64"
- Backing 46" x 64"

Tools & Supplies
- All-purpose thread to match fabrics
- Machine-quilting thread
- White machine-embroidery thread
- ½ yard 24"-wide double stick fusible web
- Basic sewing tools and supplies

Making Fence Blocks

1. Cut two 6½" x 22" strips from each blue print fat quarter; subcut two strips of one fabric into fifteen 2½" A rectangles and the two strips of the second fabric strips into twelve 2½" B rectangles.

2. From white-on-white print, cut three 10½" by fabric width strips—subcut into nine 10½" square C segments; two 6½" by fabric width strips—subcut into eighteen 2½" D segments; and two 2½" by fabric width strips—subcut into twenty-seven 2½" square E segments.

3. Draw a diagonal line from corner to corner on the wrong side of all E squares.

4. Place E on A with right sides together as shown in Figure 1; stitch on marked line. Trim seam to ¼"; press E to the right side to make an A-E unit as shown in Figure 2. Repeat for 15 A-E units.

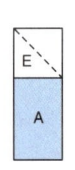

Figure 1
Place E on A with right sides together; stitch on marked line.

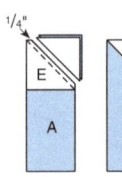

Figure 2
Trim seam to ¼"; press E to the right side to make an A-E unit.

5. Join three A-E units as shown in Figure 3; press seams in one direction.

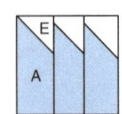

Figure 3
Join 3 A-E units.

46 Scrappy Garden Quilts   HOUSE OF WHITE BIRCHES, BERNE, INDIANA 46711   WWW.WhiteBirches.com

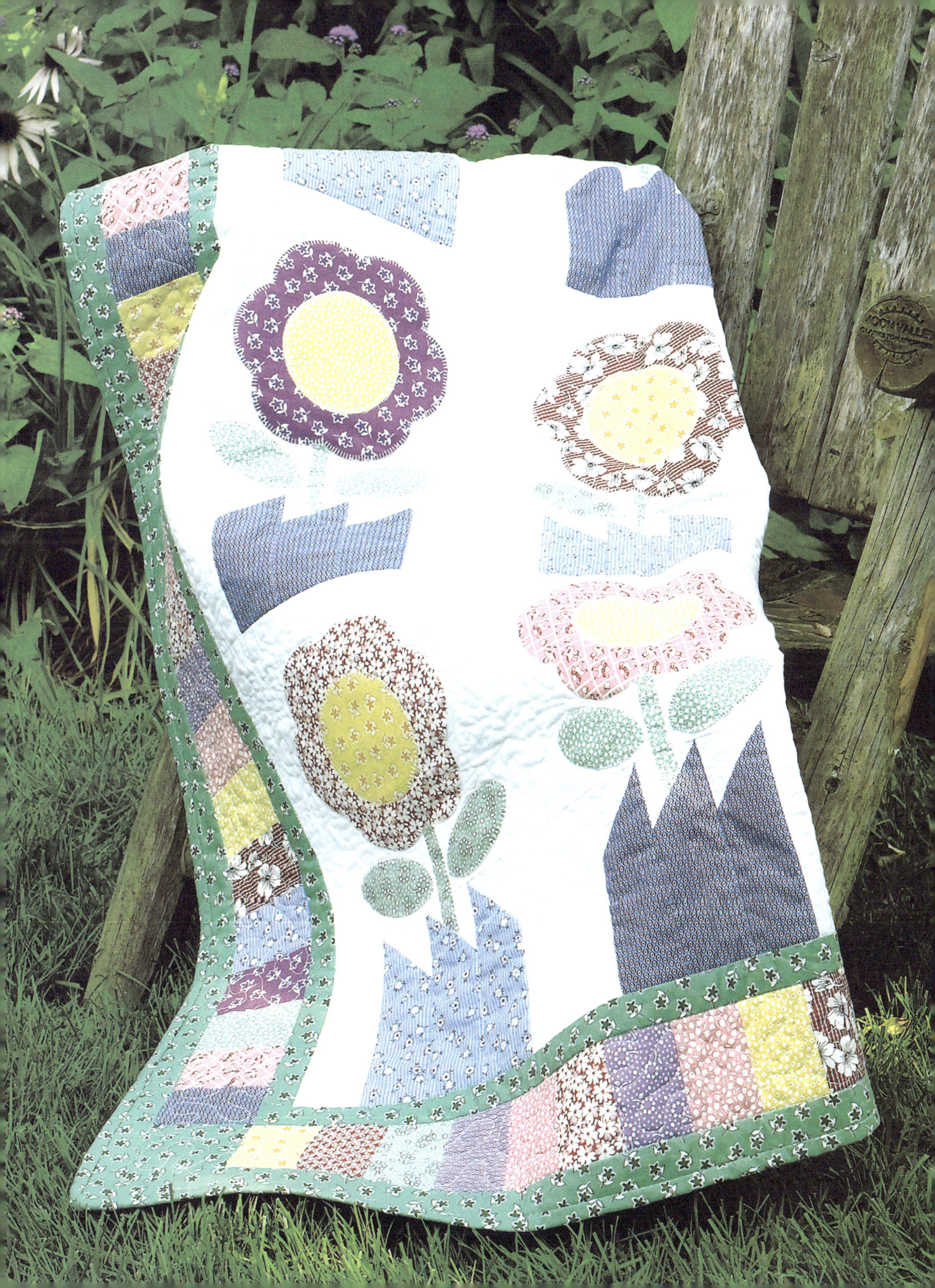

MY GARDEN PATH

6. Sew D to each side of the pieced unit to complete a left fence base as shown in Figure 4; repeat for five units.

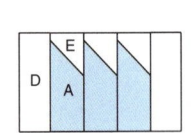

Figure 4
Sew D to each side of the pieced unit to complete a left fence base.

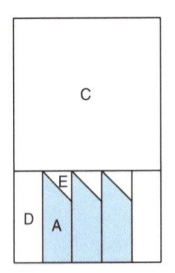

Figure 5
Sew C to the top of the A-D-E unit to make a left fence unit.

7. Sew C to the top of each unit as shown in Figure 5; press seams toward C.

8. Repeat with B, E and D pieces to make four right fence bases as shown in Figure 6. Sew C to the top of each unit and press seams toward C as shown in Figure 7.

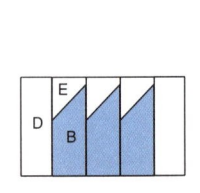

Figure 6
Make 4 right fence B-D-E bases.

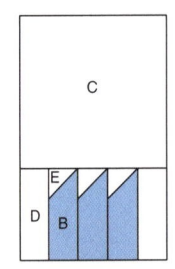

Figure 7
Sew C to the top of the B-D-E unit to complete a right fence unit.

9. Trace appliqué shapes given onto one paper side of the fusible web as directed on patterns for number to cut of each piece.

10. Cut out shapes, leaving a margin around each one; remove one paper backing and fuse to the wrong side of fabrics as directed on patterns for color. Cut out shapes on traced lines; remove paper backing.

Left Fence Flower
10" x 16" Block
Make 5

Right Fence Flower
10" x 16" Block
Make 4

11. Refer to the Placement Diagram and block drawings to arrange one each stem (right or left angled), flower and flower center, and two leaves on each left and right fence unit; when satisfied with positioning, fuse shapes in place.

12. Using white machine-embroidery thread in the top of the machine and all-purpose thread in the bobbin, machine buttonhole-stitch around each fused shape to complete the blocks.

Completing the Top

1. Arrange blocks in three rows of three blocks each referring to the Placement Diagram for positioning of right- and left-facing blocks.

2. Join blocks in rows; press seams in one direction. Join rows to complete the pieced center; press seams in one direction.

3. Cut (and piece) two 1½" x 48½" F strips and two 1½" x 32½" G strips medium green print. Sew the F strips to opposite sides and the G strips to the top and bottom of the pieced center; press seams toward strips.

4. Cut two 2½" x 22" strips from each of the fat-quarter prints. Join five strips with right sides together along length, alternating sewing direction to keep the resulting strip set from

48 Scrappy Garden Quilts HOUSE OF WHITE BIRCHES, BERNE, INDIANA 46711 WWW.WhiteBirches.com

getting wavy; press seams in one direction. Repeat for six strip sets.

5. Subcut strip sets into 3½" segments as shown in Figure 8; you will need 30 segments.

Figure 8
Subcut strip sets into 3½" segments.

6. Join segments to make two 25-piece H border strips and two 16-piece J border strips as shown in Figure 9; press.

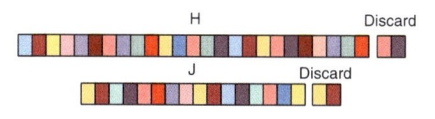

Figure 9
Join segments to make two 25-piece H border strips and two 16-piece J border strips.

7. Cut four 3½" x 3½" K squares medium green print.

8. Sew the H border strips to opposite long sides of the pieced center; press seams toward H.

9. Sew K to each end of each J strip as shown in Figure 10; press seams toward J. Sew a J-K strip to the top and bottom of the pieced center; press seams toward strips.

Figure 10
Sew K to each end of each J strip.

10. Cut (and piece) two 1½" x 40½" M strips and two 1½" x 56½" L strips medium green print. Sew L to opposite long sides and M to the top and bottom to complete the top; press seams toward M and L strips.

Finishing the Quilt

1. Sandwich batting between the completed top and prepared backing piece; pin or baste layers together to hold flat for quilting.

2. Quilt as desired by hand or machine. *Note: The quilt shown was professionally machine-quilted in an allover design using white machine-quilting thread.*

3. When quilting is complete, trim batting and backing even with quilted top; remove pins or basting; round corners using a plate as a pattern, if desired.

4. Cut five 2¼" by fabric width strips medium green print; join strips on short ends to make one long strip for binding.

5. Fold the binding strip in half along length with wrong sides together; press.

6. Sew binding strip to quilt edge with raw edges matching, mitering corners and overlapping beginning and end; turn to backside. Hand- or machine-stitch in place. ∎

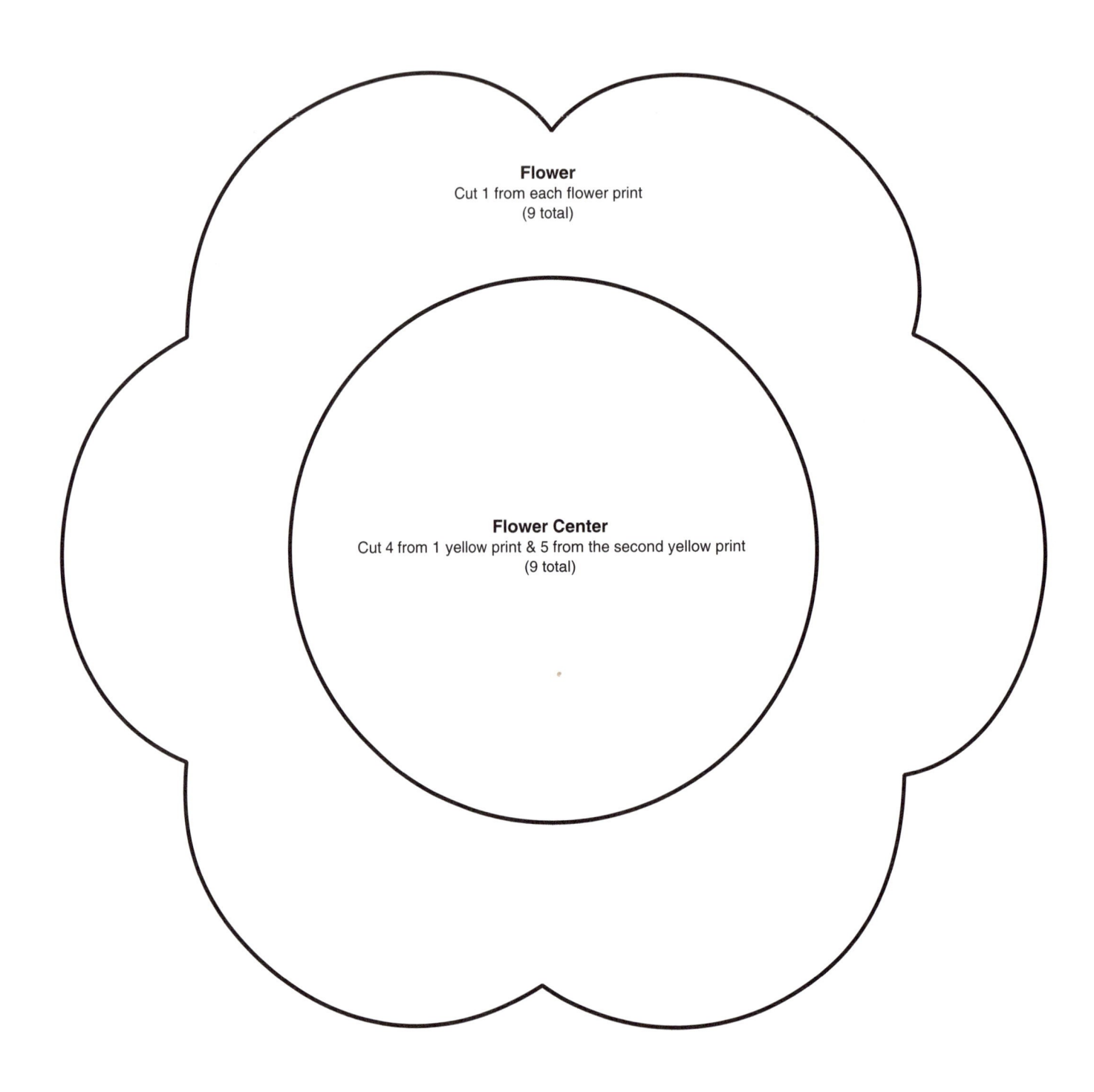

MY GARDEN PATH

Flower
Cut 1 from each flower print
(9 total)

Flower Center
Cut 4 from 1 yellow print & 5 from the second yellow print
(9 total)

Stem
Cut 5 from 1 green print
Reverse and cut 4 from the second green print
(9 total)

Leaf
Cut 10 from 1 green print & 8 from the second green print
(18 total)

My Garden Path
Placement Diagram
40" x 58"

HOUSE OF WHITE BIRCHES, BERNE, INDIANA 46711   WWW.WHITEBIRCHES.COM   Scrappy Garden Quilts

Tutti Frutti Tablecloth

BY CONNIE KAUFMAN

Food-print fabrics make the perfect colorful tablecloth for a summer picnic.

Project Specifications
Quilt Size: 72" x 72"
Block Size: 21½" x 21½" and 12" x 12"
Number of Blocks: 4 and 20

Fabric & Batting
- ½ yard apple print
- ½ yard raspberry print
- ⅔ yard strawberry print
- ⅞ yard watermelon print
- 1 yard multi-fruit print
- 1½ yards blueberry print
- 2 yards banana print
- Backing 78" x 78"
- Batting 78" x 78"

Tools & Supplies
- Neutral color all-purpose thread
- Quilting thread
- Basic sewing tools and supplies

Instructions
Making Half-Pineapple Blocks

1. Cut eight strips multi-fruit print and 12 strips banana print 3¼" by fabric width.

2. Cut one 5½" and two 6" by fabric width strips blueberry print. From the strips, cut four 5½" x 5½" squares for A and twelve 6" x 6" squares for B from the strips.

Half-Pineapple
21½" x 2½" Block

3. Mark a line from corner to corner on the wrong side of each B square.

4. Sew the four A squares to a multi-fruit print strip referring to Figure 1; press and trim to make four units.

Figure 1
Sew the 4 A squares to a strip.

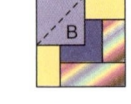

Figure 2
Place a B square on corner and stitch on marked line.

5. Sew the four units to a multi-fruit print strip in the same fashion; press and trim. Repeat to add two banana print strips.

6. Place a B square right sides together on the banana print corner and stitch on marked line as shown in Figure 2. Trim seam to ¼"; press B to the right side as shown in Figure 3.

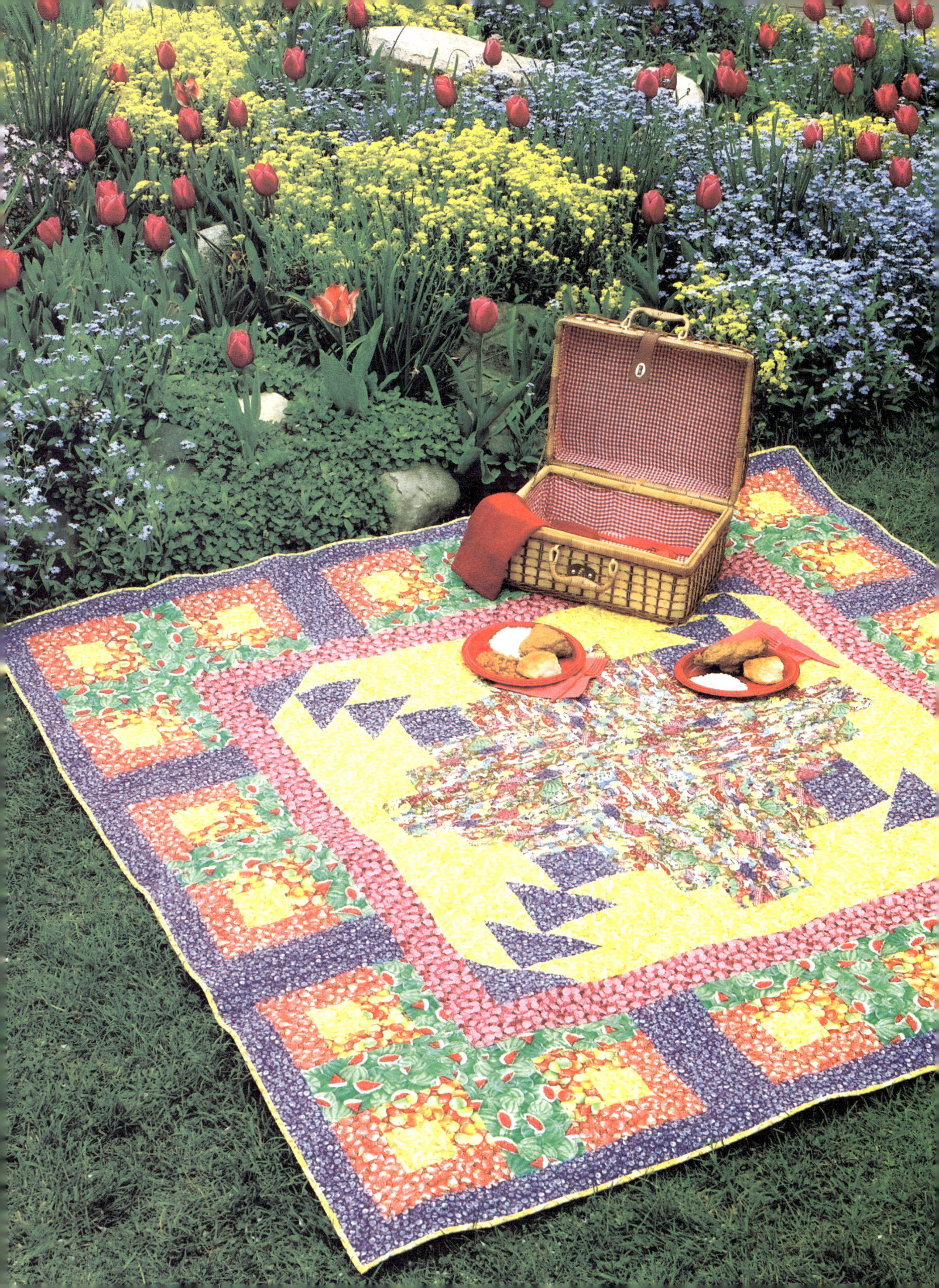

TUTTI FRUTTI TABLECLOTH

7. Continue adding multi-fruit and banana print strips to the unit and adding B to the banana print corners in the same manner to complete one Half-Pineapple block as shown in Figure 4.

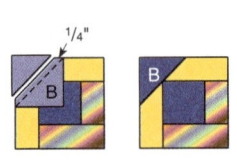

Figure 3
Trim seam to ¼"; press B to the right side.

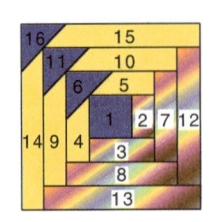

Figure 4
Complete block as shown.

8. Join the blocks referring to the Placement Diagram for positioning; press seams in opposite directions.

9. Cut (and piece) two 3" x 43½" C and two 3" x 48½" D strips raspberry print. Sew C to opposite sides and D to the top and bottom of the pieced center; press seams toward strips. Set aside.

Making Log Cabin Blocks

1. Cut two 3½" by fabric width strips banana print; subcut strips into 3½" square segments for E. You will need 20 E squares.

2. Cut the following 2¾" by fabric width strips; five apple, seven strawberry, nine watermelon and 12 blueberry prints.

3. Construct 20 Log Cabin blocks referring to Figure 5 for color and piecing order.

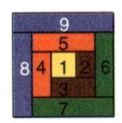

Log Cabin
12" x 12"

Figure 5
Complete Log Cabin blocks in color and number order as shown.

Figure 6
Join 4 Log Cabin blocks to make a side row.

Completing the Top

1. Join four Log Cabin blocks to make a side row referring to Figure 6; repeat for two rows. Press seams in one direction. Sew a side row to opposite sides of the bordered center; press seams toward C.

2. Join six Log Cabin blocks to make a top row referring to the Placement Diagram; repeat for bottom row. Join rows to the pieced center to complete the top; press seams toward D.

Finishing the Quilt

1. Prepare quilt top for quilting and quilt referring to the General Instructions. *Note: The sample quilt was machine-quilted in an allover pattern using yellow thread in the yellow areas and green thread in remaining areas.*

2. When quilting is complete, trim batting and backing edges even with the quilted top.

3. Prepare 8½ yards banana print binding and bind edges of quilt. ■

Tutti Frutti Tablecloth
Placement Diagram 72" x 72"

54 Scrappy Garden Quilts   HOUSE OF WHITE BIRCHES, BERNE, INDIANA 46711   WWW.WHITEBIRCHES.COM

Stained Glass Garden

BY JUDITH SANDSTROM

Floral-color fabrics work together with the black strips to create a stained glass look.

Project Specifications
Quilt Size: 18½" x 22½"

Fabric & Batting
- ⅛ –¼ yard or scraps dark blue, light and dark rose, light and dark green, gold and yellow prints or tone-on-tones
- ¼ yard light blue print for appliqué and binding
- ¼ yard bright floral for border
- ⅞ yard white-on-white print for background and backing
- Batting 23" x 27"

Tools & Supplies
- Black and white all-purpose thread
- 1 yard fusible web
- 9 yards ³⁄₁₆"-wide black rayon leadline tape
- Tacky fabric glue
- Basic sewing tools and supplies and erasable fabric marker or pencil

Appliqué
1. Prewash and iron all fabrics before cutting.

2. From white-on-white print, cut an 18" x 22" rectangle for the background and a 23" x 27" rectangle for backing; set backing piece aside. Fold background piece in quarters and crease to mark the center.

3. Prepare templates for pattern pieces using the pattern given for one-quarter of the full-size design. Arrange templates by color.

4. Place templates right side down on the paper side of the fusible web; trace as directed on the pattern for number to cut, keeping the same color pieces together in sections. Reverse pieces as directed on patterns.

5. Cut pieces apart in sections, leaving a margin around each section. Fuse sections to the wrong side of fabrics as directed on patterns for color. Cut out shapes on traced lines; remove paper backing.

6. Copy the whole one-quarter pattern on paper. Center the pattern on the wrong side of the background; pin to hold. Tape to a window or use a light box and transfer the complete design to the background, moving the paper pattern to other quarters of the background when finished with one area and using an erasable fabric marker or pencil.

STAINED GLASS GARDEN

7. Arrange and pin shapes on the marked background referring to the marked lines, pattern and Placement Diagram for positioning. *Note: Pieces will be touching but not overlapping except where marked on pattern. There should be a ¼" seam allowance on the background outer edges.*

8. When satisfied with placement, fuse shapes in place referring to manufacturer's instructions.

9. After all pieces have been fused, trim the background piece to 15" x 19".

10. Referring to the full-size one-quarter pattern for application order and to Using Leadline Tape, cover all edges of fused appliqué shapes with the ³⁄₁₆"-wide black leadline tape.

Completing the Top

1. Cut four 2½" x 19" strips bright floral.

2. Sew a strip to opposite long sides and a strip to the top and bottom of the appliquéd center; press seams toward strips.

Finishing

1. Sandwich batting between the completed top and prepared backing piece; pin or baste layers together to hold flat for quilting.

2. Stitch leadline tape edges to act as quilting referring to Using Leadline Tape.

3. Machine-stitch in ditch of border seams using white all-purpose thread.

4. When quilting is complete, trim batting and backing even with quilted top; remove pins or basting.

5. Cut three 2¼" by fabric width strips light blue print. Join strips on short ends to make one long strip for binding.

6. Fold the binding strip in half along length with wrong sides together; press.

7. Sew binding strip to quilt edge with raw edges matching, mitering corners and overlapping beginning and end; turn to backside. Hand- or machine-stitch in place. ■

Using Leadline Tape

Leadline tape has some advantages over fabric bias tape and is easy to use. Refer to the following hints when applying to project.

1. Stretch the tape around curved edges.

2. Manufacturer suggests searing ends with a match to prevent fraying, but in the project the ends are secured with tacky fabric glue.

3. Center the tape over the edge of the fabric to be outlined as shown in Figure 1.

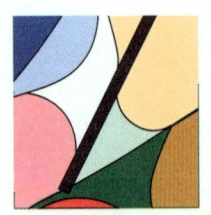

Figure 1
Center the tape over the edge of the fabric to be outlined.

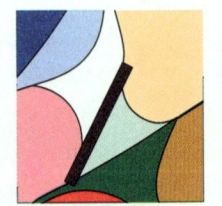

Figure 2
Cut the tape at the end so it will extend slightly over the edge of the appliqué shape.

4. Apply tacky fabric glue to the edge of the appliqué shape; center the tape over the appliqué edge and press flat. Continue adding glue as you place the tape along the edge.

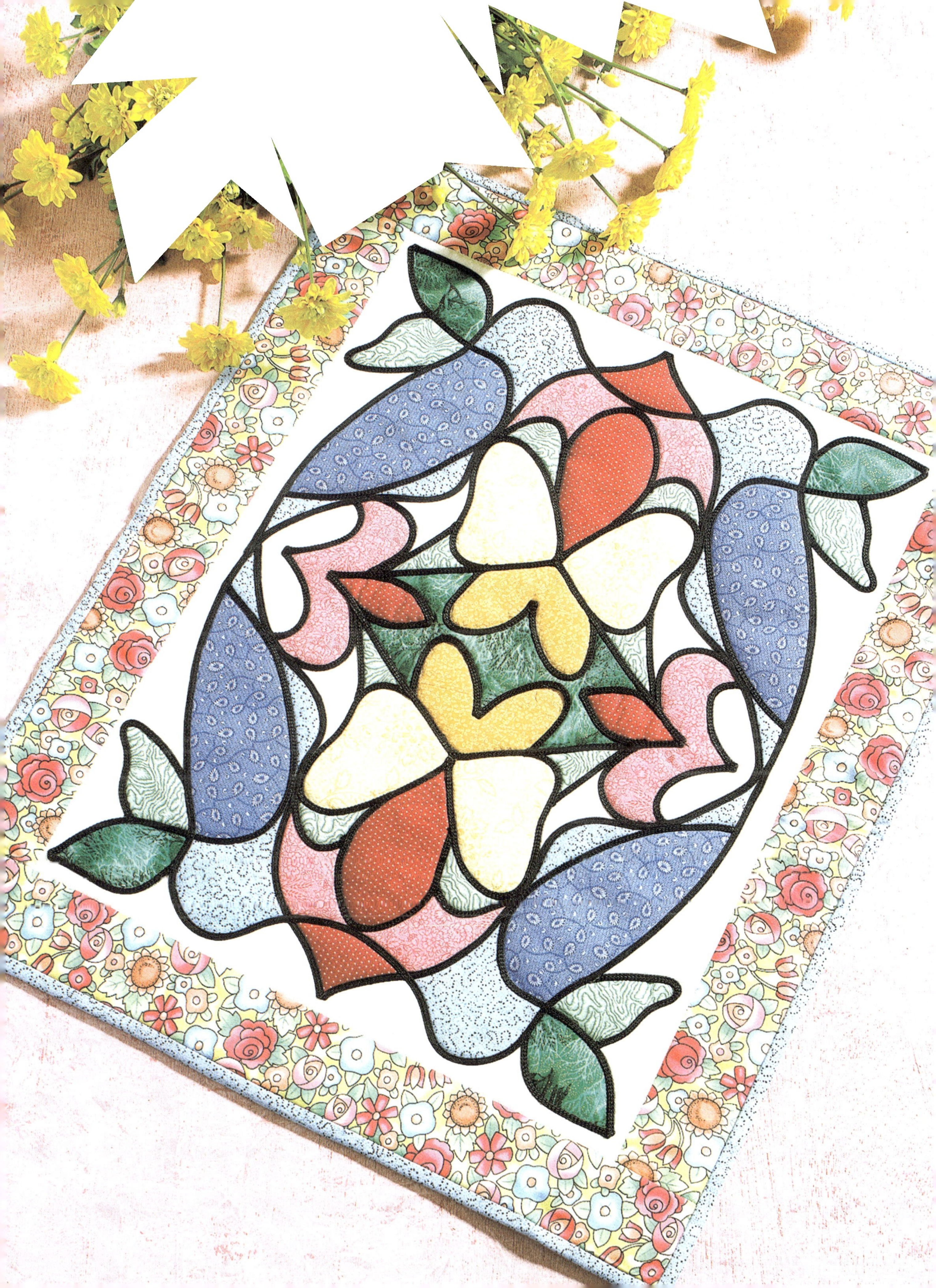

STAINED GLASS GARDEN

5. Cut the tape at the end so it will extend slightly over the edge of the appliqué shape as shown in Figure 2.

6. Start with smaller pieces and cover the ends with the next piece of tape as shown in Figure 3.

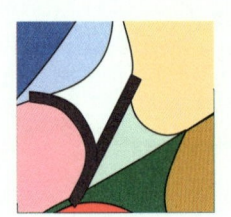

Figure 3
Cover the ends with the next piece of tape.

Figure 4
Points may be continued in 1 piece by folding the tape over itself.

7. Use a continuous piece of tape when possible in order to have fewer ends to cover.

8. Points may be continued in one piece by folding the tape over itself as shown in Figure 4.

9. Work from the center out or refer to pattern for number order.

10. Stitch on both sides of the tape using black all-purpose thread and starting in the center and working toward the outside.

11. A 2.0 twin needle may be used to stitch both edges at the same time. Use a continuous stitch whenever possible to avoid starts and stops.

Stained Glass Garden
Placement Diagram
18½" x 22½"

¼ **Appliqué Design**

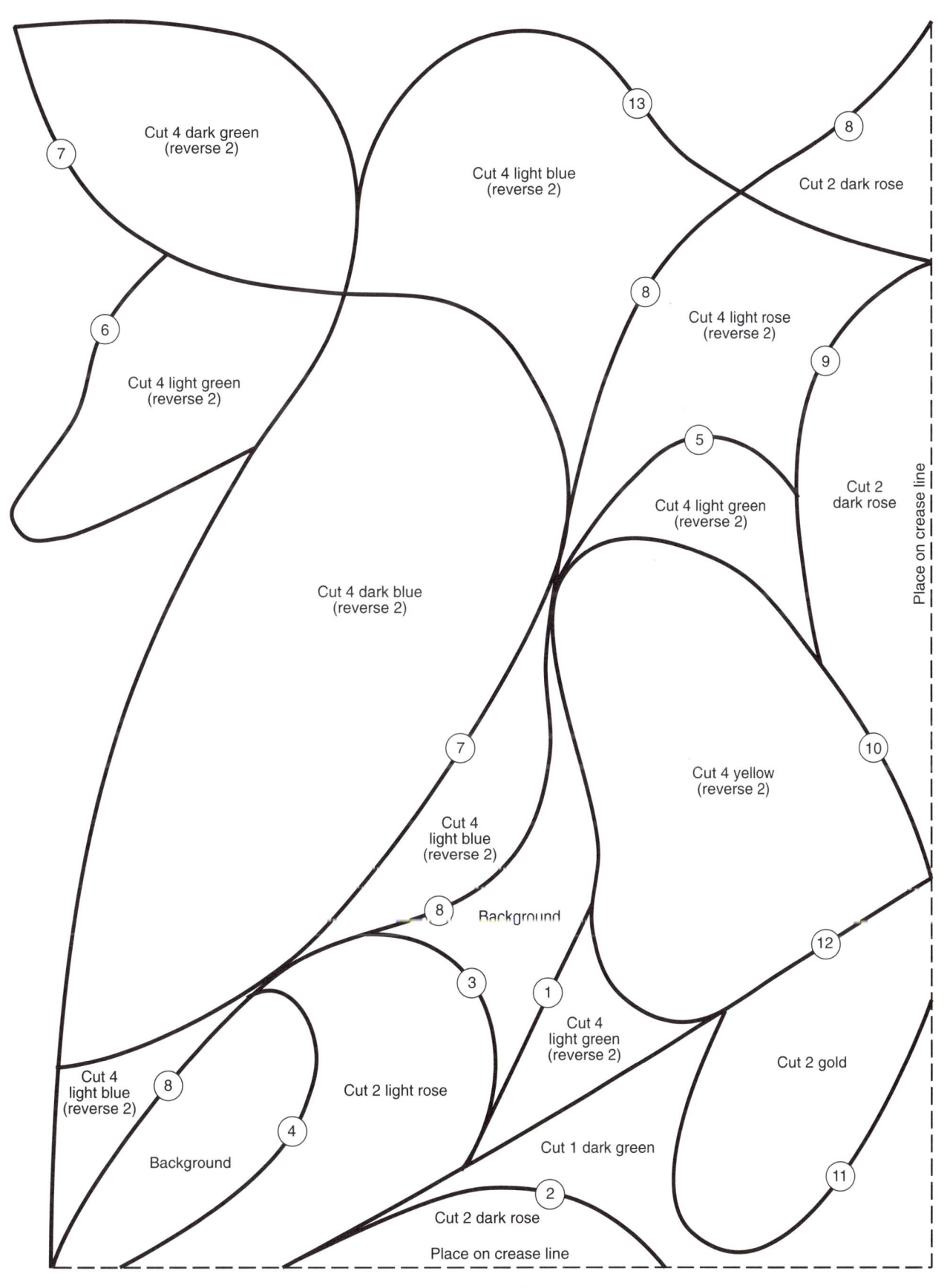

HOUSE OF WHITE BIRCHES, BERNE, INDIANA 46711   WWW.WHITEBIRCHES.COM   **Scrappy Garden Quilts** 59

Undersea Garden

BY PATSY MORELAND

Have fun adding lots of charms and jewels to this sea-theme wall quilt.

Project Specifications
Quilt Size: 22½" x 18"

Fabric & Batting
- 6" x 18" rectangle geometric print
- ¾" x 6½" strip tan felt
- ⅛ yard sand/pebble motif
- ¼ yard black print for binding
- ½ yard sea-theme fabric with fern, leaf, fish and shell motifs
- ½ yard watercolor mottled for background
- ⅝ yard blue small-wale corduroy
- ⅔ yard washable canvas
- Backing 27" x 22"
- Quilter's fleece 27" x 22"

Tools & Supplies
- All-purpose thread to match fabrics
- Clear nylon monofilament
- ½ yard double-stick fusible web
- 1 bottle craft glue
- 1 bottle silver dimensional fabric paint
- 6 (1⅛") pastel premade fabric yo-yos
- 4 (1½") dark premade fabric yo-yos
- 5 (1¼") dark premade fabric yo-yos
- 2 sea-theme buttons
- 8 sea-theme charms
- Assorted beads for "jewels"
- 1 package 5mm crystal paillette sequins
- 1 penny
- 24" quilt hanger or 4 (1") plastic rings
- Basic sewing tools and supplies, press cloth, rotary point cutter and toothpicks

Cutting
1. Cut one 11½" x 19" rectangle watercolor mottled for A.

2. Cut a 3½" x 19" strip sand/pebble motif for B.

3. Cut two strips each 2½" x 19" for C and 2½" x 18½" for D blue small-wale corduroy, cutting D along the length of the fabric.

4. Cut a 27" x 22" rectangle canvas.

Completing the Top
1. Sew A to B along the 19" edge; press seam toward A.

2. Select four shell, three fern, four fish and two leaf motifs from the sea-theme print; remove paper liner and bond fusible web to the wrong side of the motifs referring to manufacturer's instructions. **Note:** *If you cannot find one fabric with all these sea-theme motifs, you may use scraps of any fabrics with these shapes. You may also use both the right and wrong sides of the fabrics.*

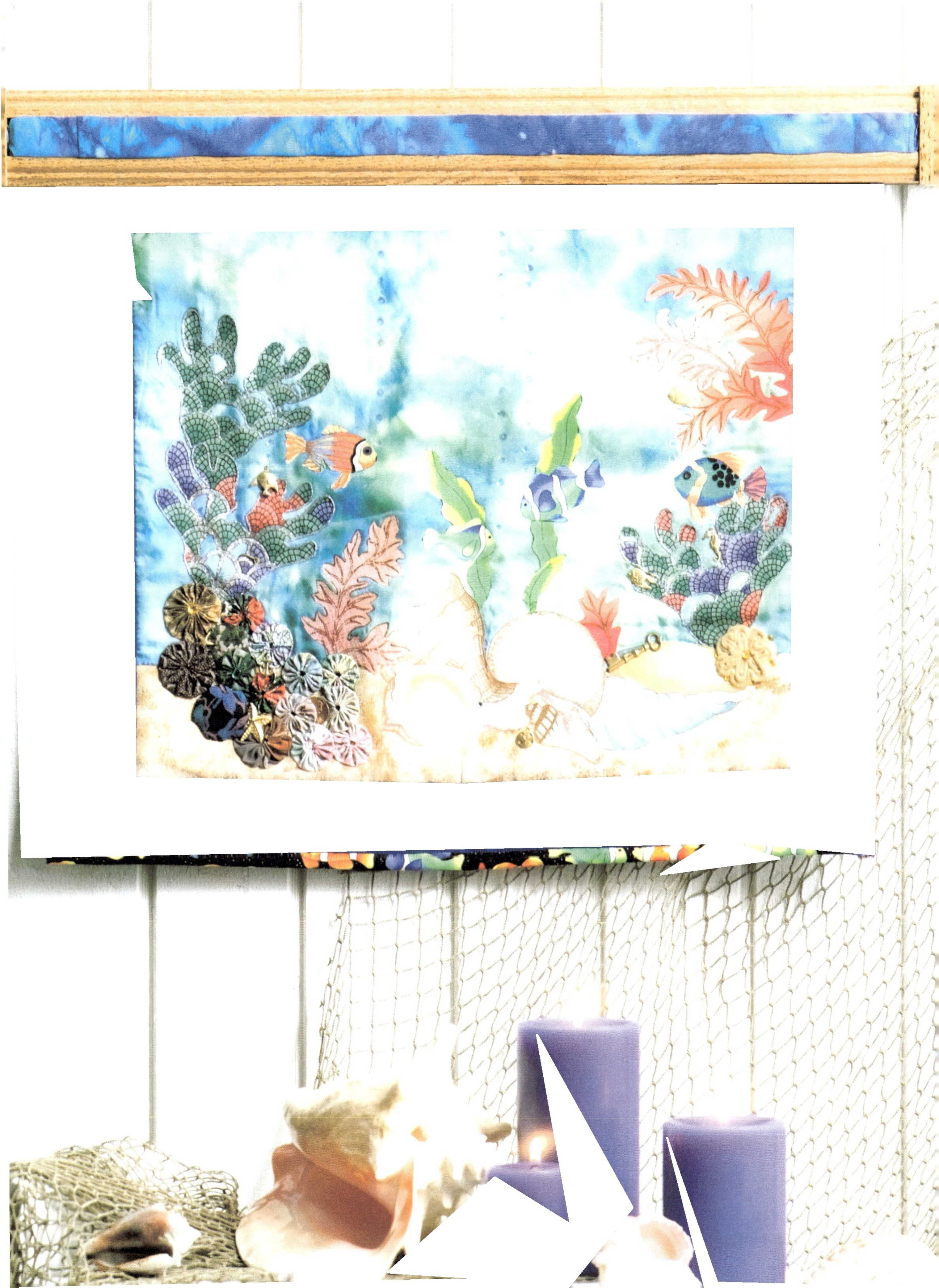

UNDERSEA GARDEN

3. Cut out shapes on motif lines; remove paper backing.

4. Bond fusible web to the wrong side of the geometric print. Prepare template for coral using pattern given; trace pattern onto the paper side of the fused fabric as directed on pattern. Cut out coral shapes on traced lines, cutting out openings with the point cutter.

5. Referring to the Placement Diagram and photo of project, arrange the cut-out motifs on the A-B background. When satisfied with arrangement, iron in place using a press cloth.

6. Sew a C strip to the top and bottom and a D strip to opposite sides of the fused top; press seams toward strips.

Finishing

1. Place the backing piece wrong side up on a flat surface; place canvas piece on top. Place quilter's fleece on top and the fused top right side up on the layers.

2. Stitch in the ditch between seams of C and D strips and the A-B background using clear nylon monofilament in the top of the machine and all-purpose thread in the bobbin.

3. Cut three 2¼" by fabric width strips black print. Join strips on short ends to make one long strip for binding.

4. Fold the binding strip in half along length with wrong sides together; press.

5. Sew binding strips to quilt edges with raw edges matching, mitering corners and overlapping beginning and end; turn to backside. Hand- or machine-stitch in place.

Embellishing

1. Create a cluster of yo-yos on the bottom left corner, placing some yo-yos with gathered side down; when satisfied with positioning, glue in place.

2. Apply glue to 5mm crystal paillette sequins using toothpicks and place from fish to the top of the A-B background to simulate bubbles coming from the fish mouths.

3. Apply glue to the penny, nine round "jewels" and charms and scatter over the top referring to the photo of the project for positioning suggestions.

4. With a single strand of knotted thread, stitch a curved line along the tan felt strip as shown in Figure 1.

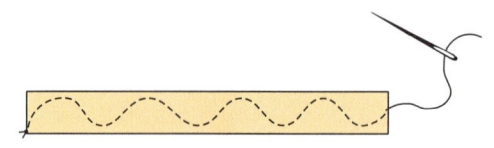

Figure 1
Stitch a curved line along the tan felt strip.

5. Pull the thread to form a circle of the strip; stitch ends together to hold to make a rosette.

6. Glue the rosette to the bottom of the right-edge coral.

7. Outline holes in coral with silver dimensional paint referring to manufacturer's instructions.

8. Evenly space the 1" plastic rings 2" from top backside edges of quilt and hand-stitch in place or hang from a 24" quilt hanger to display. ■

Undersea Garden
Placement Diagram
22½" x 18"

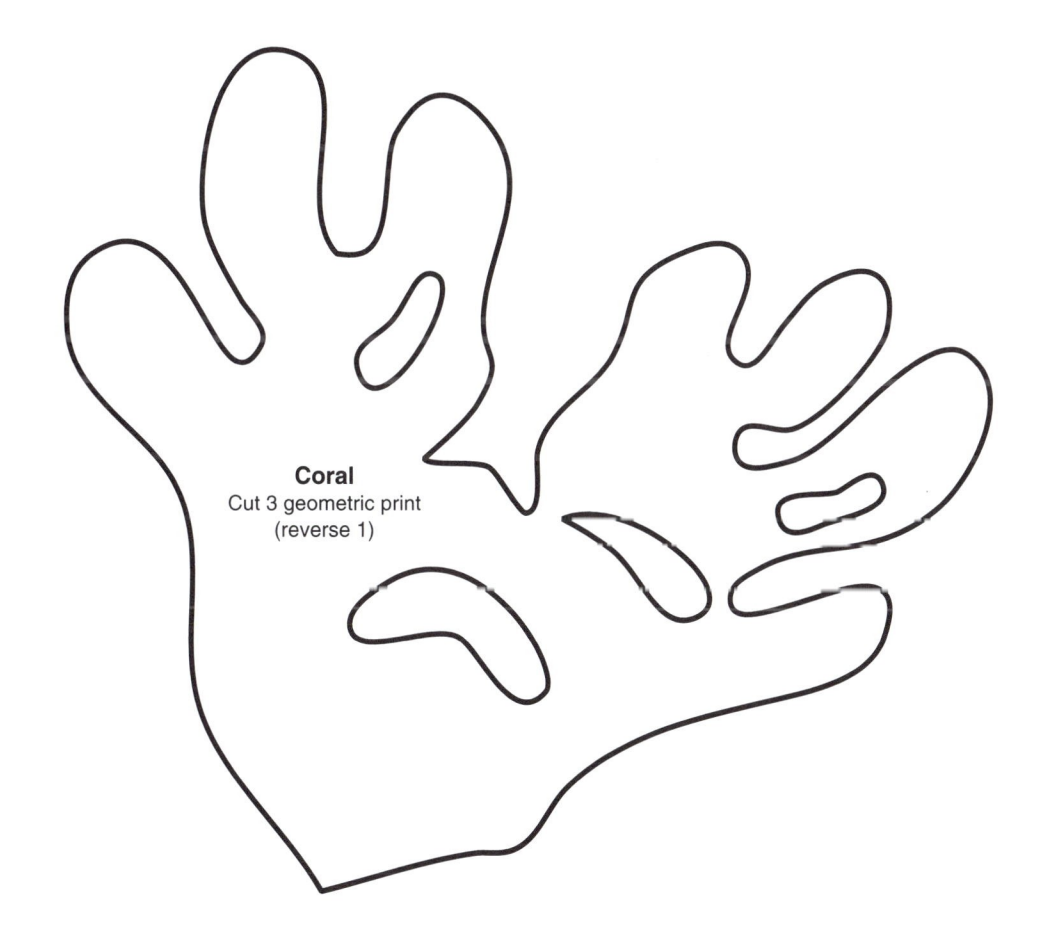

Coral
Cut 3 geometric print
(reverse 1)

Metric Conversion Charts

Metric Conversions

U.S. Measurements		Multiplied by		Metric Measurement
yards	x	.9144	=	meters (m)
yards	x	91.44	=	centimeters (cm)
inches	x	2.54	=	centimeters (cm)
inches	x	25.40	=	millimeters (mm)
inches	x	.0254	=	meters (m)

Metric Measurements		Multiplied by		U.S. Measurements
centimeters	x	.3937	=	inches
meters	x	1.0936	=	yards

Standard Equivalents

U.S. Measurement		Metric Measurement		
1/8 inch	=	3.20 mm	=	0.32 cm
1/4 inch	=	6.35 mm	=	0.635 cm
3/8 inch	=	9.50 mm	=	0.95 cm
1/2 inch	=	12.70 mm	=	1.27 cm
5/8 inch	=	15.90 mm	=	1.59 cm
3/4 inch	=	19.10 mm	=	1.91 cm
7/8 inch	=	22.20 mm	=	2.22 cm
1 inch	=	25.40 mm	=	2.54 cm
1/8 yard	=	11.43 cm	=	0.11 m
1/4 yard	=	22.86 cm	=	0.23 m
3/8 yard	=	34.29 cm	=	0.34 m
1/2 yard	=	45.72 cm	=	0.46 m
5/8 yard	=	57.15 cm	=	0.57 m
3/4 yard	=	68.58 cm	=	0.69 m
7/8 yard	=	80.00 cm	=	0.80 m
1 yard	=	91.44 cm	=	0.91 m

Embroidery Stitch Guide

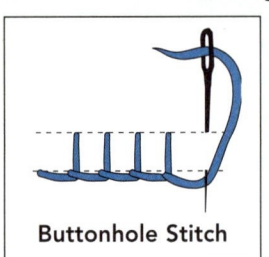

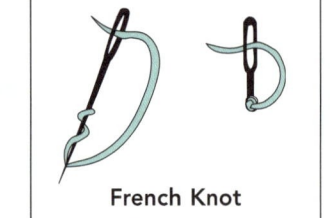

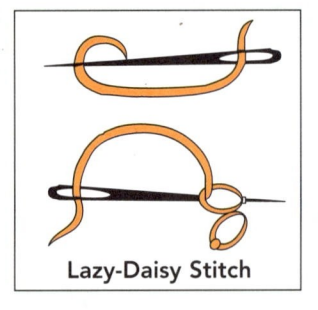

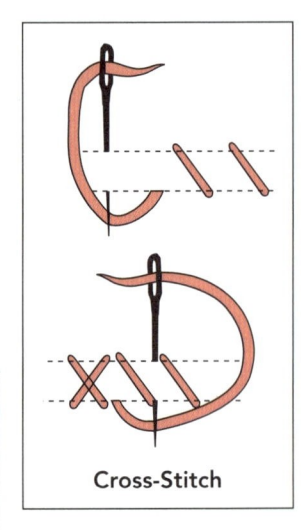

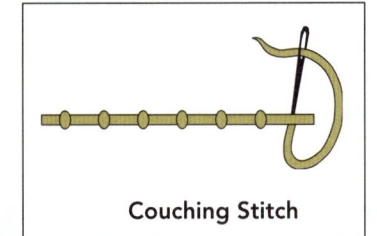

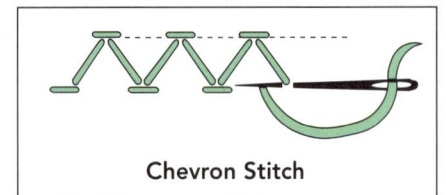

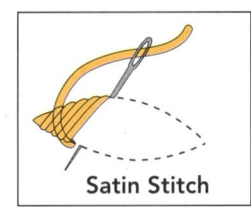

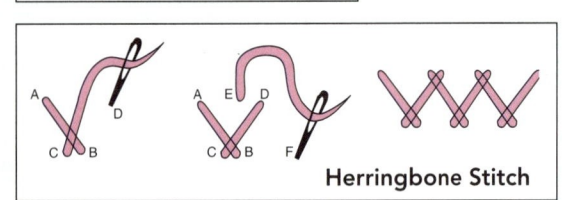

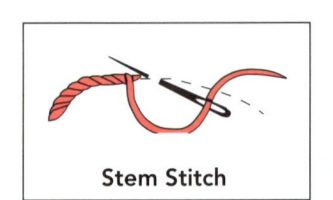

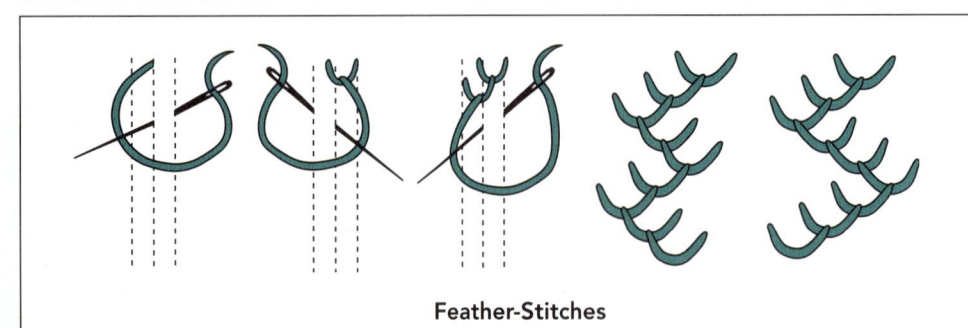

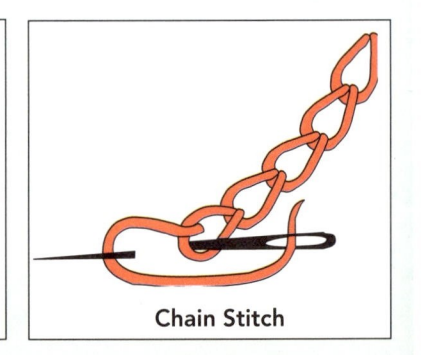

- Buttonhole Stitch
- French Knot
- Lazy-Daisy Stitch
- Cross-Stitch
- Couching Stitch
- Chevron Stitch
- Satin Stitch
- Herringbone Stitch
- Stem Stitch
- Fly Stitch
- Feather-Stitches
- Chain Stitch